# JOHN ON...

## REFLECTIONS ON AN
## UNUSUAL GOSPEL

# John on...

## Reflections on an Unusual Gospel

Terry Young

# DEDICATION

To Steve and Dee Sturman and many years of friendship.

# PREFACE

I'm never sure of the difference between a preface and the acknowledgments, or indeed whether a preface replaces an introduction or complements it in some other way. So, as I try to wrap up the first draft and before I dive into the many comments that have come back to for clarification, correction or deletion, I wanted to thank those who have given me the appetite for gospels such as John's and the confidence to believe that anyone can get a lot out of reading and studying the text.

My parents were missionaries when I first knew them and then strangers in a strange land as they settled in the West Midlands and I went through my teenage years and into my twenties. In the Middle East we were never part of the expatriate set, were readily identifiable as foreigners, and worshipped mainly with people from Kerala who had moved to what is now the UAE to work in the banks and commercial sector. The weather was warm and the culture warmer, so we enjoyed our life as outsiders mixing in. In 1970s England, large families were characteristic of immigrants and the unemployed and, with our weird accents and mission income, we were readily identified as having a foot in each camp. For these and other reasons, I guess I identify as an outsider more readily than anything else.

A consistent thread throughout all this was my parents' focus on reading scripture and praying – on their own, together, and with us – and basing their decisions on what they understood as a result. Most people who came through our home (and there were visiting diners several times a week and overnight guests more than once a month) also had an angle to share on faith.

I guess my adult years have consisted of discovering that much of what I took for granted growing up was rather rare in society at large, and much that I thought exotic growing up was common. I can never, of course, see the world again through the same eyes I once had when we first arrived in Birmingham. However, what I hope to pass on is the rather rare idea that the Bible works every day and was written for ordinary people to read, digest, and get something from. You need not be a specialist, but learning is as expensive as it has always been because it is paid for primarily in time – the one quantity that we each receive at exactly the same rate.

So then, I would like to thank those who have spent time reviewing these chapters as they have come off the press: Alison Brook, Alistair Hornal, Dave Baldwin, Dee Molton, Des Dummett and Jo McNamara. In very different ways, they have all contributed to what you have before you today. Dave, in particular, has helped me with the theological terrain I have passed through as a tourist. So, thank you all!

I would also like to thank Tony Gray of WORDS BY DESIGN for design work and everything else related to publishing.

And finally, a big thank-you to Dani for hanging in there while I have been tap-tap-tapping away in the kitchen. For providing the security for me to be this irresponsible – thank you!

Datchet, 2018

# CONTENTS

Preface          vii

Introduction          1

John on… The Word          7
John on… The Father          19
John on… The Spirit          31
John on… Belief          43
John on… Signs          55
John on… I Am          67
John on… Glory          79
John on… Light and Darkness          89
John on… The Hour          99
John on… One to One          111
John on… The Disciples          121
John on… The Rulers          133
John on… The Crowd          145
John on… The World          155
John on… Evidence          167

Epilogue          183

About the Author          186

Indices          187

# INTRODUCTION

If this book works for you, I hope it will be quite unlike anything else you have read, and the reason is that the best bits aren't in the book – some of them haven't even been written yet. Those will be the ones you work on for yourself out of the sheer enjoyment of reading and reflecting on John. And the very best bits are those John first put on paper. This book is simply aimed at getting you closer to the original.

John's gospel is quite unlike anything I have ever read and I would not be surprised if you have found the same thing. One need not have read this gospel deeply or even frequently to be aware that it is different from the others: many favourite stories about Jesus are not in there, while John reports scenes, conversations, miracles and tragedies that we do not find elsewhere. But it is not so much the what that draws us in, but the way he plays with themes, drawing them together, teasing them apart, holding them up to the light and helping us to catch colours that we never imagined were in there.

If it works for you, *John on...* will help you to capture a sense of discovery and excitement in John and, I hope, the confidence to continue mining his material for yourself. It's not so much about the gospel, or even about enjoying the gospel, although I hope it contributes to your experience on both fronts. It is about building confidence that anyone can mine gold from this gospel.

As a child, I remember having this idea that the Bible had two types of writing – collections of single verses that you memorised, and longer passages that your parents would read out or tell you about. I do not know how long I held this rather vague idea but it is not hard to see why – there seemed to be verses that made sense and were worth remembering on their own, and other passages that contained a flow of a story and made more sense as part of a greater whole. Years later, I remember one of the elders at the church where I went as a teenager, Neale Brinkley, explaining in his series on 2 Corinthians that the letter was *studded*, but not *studied*. By that he meant that there were lots of glittering texts in territory that was seldom trodden. It was a brilliant insight and listening in a single sitting to David Suchet reading 2 Corinthians, I was drawn again to reflect on what a profound observation it was.

I love verses, but I also love chapters and books and the whole shebang! Our western churches have, in my view, carried the analogy of finding nuggets too far and have focused too much on the nuggets, so that we have made Bible study too great an exercise in extracting nice verses from their context in order to build three-point sermons.

The trouble with mining is that it is a skilled operation that involves massive pieces of equipment, engineering, geology, mineralogy, hydrology and a dozen other skills… plus all the sweat and danger experienced by those in the front line. A few people may pan in their spare time for gold if they live near a river, but mining, on the whole, is a campaign best left to the experts.

To shift the analogy back to John, we expect to pay our experts – the professional Christian at the front on a Sunday – to train and do the hard work, so that we can sit back and watch in wonder. We love the glitter but we feel we lack the tools, the training and the time to set out in search of gold for ourselves.

I hope in the following chapters to persuade you that you can get gold out of 'them thar hills.' There are streams flowing from this gospel that you can dip your sieve into and catch something amazing every time. John's *Spirit of Truth* (John 16:12) is still out and about to guide you and bring good stuff your way. More than anything else, that should encourage you to dip into the book for yourself.

And there is something else for us in our information-rich environment – we can reach knowledge and analysis that would have once taken days or even decades to acquire. There is lots of stuff in the river of information that you will want to filter out, but there is gold in there, too, and you can grab it all with the click of a mouse.

When printing made the Bible cheap enough for ordinary people to buy their own copies, they read and became experts. The experience of faith and the expertise needed to practise it was wrested from official groups and handled with joy and awe by ordinary people. In our era, we have handed our treasure back to professionals to look after, while we focus on the day-to-day demands of making ends meet, raising our families, looking after our loved ones, or making our own professional progress in a different field. The internet allows us all to be true amateurs once more, becoming experts out of the sheer love of learning.

Given the Spirit to guide and so much access to material, I want to encourage you to get into John for yourself. You, too, can become an expert in time, and be rewarded in the meantime for the effort you make.

I hope that the chapters ahead will help you see little of how I have gone about this project and encourage you to step out on your own. I first started pulling questions together to study John – chapter by chapter in that case – close to 30 years ago, and the quality of the discussions that emerged persuaded me that the quality of the questions was not terribly important. If you could make them sufficiently open, people would contribute and everyone would learn something.

The time frames are not always clear, since I have not gone back to put all my stories in chronological order. I'm sorry if this drives you wild, but when I tell you about something that happened last week, it may have happened several years ago by now. I hope the freshness overcomes the frustration.

For me, the passage of time explains a lot of the depth in John's writing. He seems to be a very old man looking back, summing up decades of reflection, and piecing together the extraordinary scenes and memories of the most extraordinary life. There is instant gratification in his gospel, but there is also a richness that matures, like the grapes in John 15, from season to season. So, the sooner you can get started, the better. And like a pension, the earlier you start, the better it is at the end.

I haven't built a massive library about John. I like Don Carson's *IVP* commentary on John (mine is more than a quarter of a century old, now) but there is lots of material out there. I like the way he balances the evidence, and gives a clear view of the options in the original languages. I also liked his triplet of sonnets in the middle of his commentary on John 14. I have also bought beyond my reading so that a three-part commentary by JC Ryle stands unread on a bookshelf. There are lots of others from which to choose. I have also found plenty of material on the web – systematic and illustrational – and particularly liked the material that Dr Felix Just SJ has posted on John's writings (http://catholic-resources.org/John/index.html). You may warm to or veer away from his theology, but that is not my point. As a teacher, he produces lucid and full notes and I have found them very helpful.

Perhaps it is worth commenting a little on how you might go about using material on the web. I had been raving about Bible Hub at church one Sunday and got an email enquiry a few days later from someone who had tried it out and had eventually come across an advert for a particular translation of the Bible. The question was, did I think the person should go for it? This raises a couple of interesting questions if you are keen, as I am, that Christians should use the web much more in their Bible study. When you recommend a site, how much are you recommending? What about the dangers that some who might follow your example lack the judgement needed to do so safely?

To make the most of what is on offer, I would suggest you avoid both fear and naivety. If you only look at sources you agree with, there will usually be plenty on offer, but you will struggle to become the approved workman that Paul wrote about (2 Timothy 2:15).

There is plenty of scholarship and thoughtful Christianity out there being produced by people who love Jesus, but maybe not quite in the way that you do. Don't be naïve, either – instead, try to develop an eye for the extremist, the person who wants to explore just half the argument, the writer who is a little too eager to have an argument. And, above all, pray regularly about what you are learning. Like any amateur, I have picked up the tools that work best for me and acquired a measure of competence with them. I am sure you will do the same.

I take a very traditional line on John: that it was written by the eponymous disciple, who wrote the three letters that we also have in the New Testament, and also wrote Revelation. When you get to grips with John, you may or may not be persuaded of this position. I won't worry too much either way, so long as you have been touched by the magical narrative.

Now, what will you make of John?

Once you have worked your way through this, there is an even more interesting question you might like to turn your mind to: what would he have made of you?

# 1 | JOHN ON… THE WORD

In the beginning was the Word. (John 1:1)

Most of us encounter the opening bars of John's masterpiece at Advent, often at a Carol Service, sometimes in our private devotions as we seek something special to set this Christmas apart from others. I remember being moved by the local bishop speaking simply on this passage during a Midnight Eucharist at Clive Church in Shropshire more than a decade ago, looking down from a balcony, as I recall, and enjoying the acoustics of a grand old building. And there is certainly a resonant quality to John's prologue, catching not least an echo of the first line of the book of Genesis – you need not have much of an ear to sense that something momentous and mysterious is unfolding.

By the end of his gospel (John 21:25), John sees so many words that the world itself, the world into which Jesus came and which did not know him at the start, might overflow with books about him. And in between, there is a recurring tussle over the writings – principally by Moses and the prophets – between Jesus, the Word, and the guardians of the writings who in John's narrative are predominantly the Pharisees. This tussle is full of words, shot through with debate and dialectic – passages that I find hard to follow and in which I realise that I am watching people whose outlook and sense of reason is very different from anything I have grown up with.

There is plenty of material on the web and in most commentaries on John to fill you in on how John has blended Greek and Jewish thinking when he uses the word, 'Word', and the neat way he has poured it into a Christian context. I do not plan to dive into any of this – first, because you can get to it as easily as I can, and second, it is quite technical in places and nothing makes you look like an idiot more than a terminological slip when discussing something you are not fully on top of. You rarely do well trying to explain things you don't fully understand.

In the era before crystal oscillators brought us digital timekeeping, I had to write an essay on time. Mechanical clocks have something called *the escapement* which counts the swings of a pendulum on a grandfather clock or the spins of a balance wheel in a watch. I found a diagram but could not make much sense it and sort of muddled through (these days there are shedloads of accessible articles and videos online). When the essay came back, my tutor had left a note next to my diagram, explaining that he couldn't really understand that piece of the essay. And as soon as I read it, I knew why – I hadn't understood it either.

## The Communicating Word

So let's turn to concepts that we *are* able to follow. Words are for communication – we all know about the 'send' button that fires off our email, confirms the order or downloads a book onto our eBook reader. We say that we live in a connected world, and whether we are ordering our groceries, chatting with our grandchildren, or finding out about something new, we are aware how digital networks have transformed our world.

And, as it turns out, one of John's big ideas is about sending and being sent. There is lots of sending in John's gospel: priests and Levites are sent to John the Baptist (John 1:19), John the Baptist himself declares that he has been sent ahead of the Christ (John 3:28); the authorities send officers to arrest Jesus (John 7:32), while Mary and Martha send Jesus an 'SOS' when their brother Lazarus is dying (John 11:3). There is even a pun about sending in the story of the blind man (John 9:7). But the biggest idea is that God sent Jesus, not only as a messenger, but as the message.

At church this year, we have decided to get as many people reading through the New Testament as possible and so there was a reading plan circulated on yellow paper at the turn of the year. Neither of us is very good at looking after paper (or houseplants), and so my wife downloaded her own plan and I decided to try reading in Greek using Bible Hub. I did a little classical Greek at school, and after scraping an 'O'-Level – and it really was scraping through – I spent early mornings once a week with my classics teacher, working through Mark. The experience this time has been wonderfully different because I have not tried to get the grammar sorted out – it is all there if I need it, most of it only a click away.

So I've tried to get a feel for the words and move quickly, rather than accurately, supported by a reasonable recollection of the English text, gleaned from a variety of translations over the years. In terms of how good a reader I am, let's say similar to a five or six-year-old trying to get to grips with a book in English. This relaxed incompetence leaves me free to have fun. I tried to read Jude's letter recently, and it is full of complicated words, so that I spent nearly all my time on the English translation. John's writing, however, is a bit like that of Dr Seuss – he of *The Cat in the Hat* – with lots of phrases that repeat over and over again. Once you have 'Amen' repeated, you know that there will be something like, 'I say to you,' or even one of the 'I am' sayings. In other places, John repeats similar ideas in different ways, layering them up, visiting and revisiting them, all of which makes John easy to read and, paradoxically, hard to understand – which adds to the attraction.

One of John's sending words sounds like our word for apostle – *apostello* – someone who has been sent. It appears 133 times in the New Testament (NT) according to Strong's concordance which I accessed online and just over a fifth of those are in John. The other word he uses as he opens his gospel – *pempo* – is less frequent and I cannot think of an English equivalent. There are also variants but, one way or another, there are almost three references to sending or being sent per chapter throughout this gospel.

One of the things that caught my eye as I read is the use of participles – I think I have that right – where the Father, for instance, is, 'the having sent me one' (John 6:38, 39) or even the 'having sent me Father' (John 14:24). It is an elegant and compact way of capturing an idea but it does mean you need to know loads of grammar, which is why I prefer to ride the Bible Hub train rather than walk the distance. It is Eastertide as I write and, ironically, I spent many Easter holidays from school memorising French, Latin or Greek nouns and verbs for the coming exams. It was a disappointment first time round, so I'm just having fun now.

The relationship between Jesus as the one sent and the Father as the one who sends underscores an important element of who the Word is – not just a messenger (although certainly a messenger) but the message itself. This identification is very direct, for 'whatever the Father does the Son also does' (John 5:19b) and whoever has seen Jesus has seen the one sending him: whether someone in the crowd or one of the disciples (John 12:45; 14:9). There are questions at the end that may help you pursue this idea.

**The Word and the Writings**

So what is the connection – or maybe it is easier to identify the differences – between this messenger-message and other messengers with their messages? As we consider the pattern of arguments throughout John's gospel – swathes of John 5, 6, 7, 8, the second halves of John 10 and 12 – we realise that the connection between what was written and what Jesus represents is at the heart of the debate. Jesus claims to have one relationship with the writings, while the establishment claims to have another, and these claims are such that they cannot both be right. It all comes to a head from John 18 onward and, finally, in more words as Pilate publishes the solution in Aramaic, Latin and Greek: 'Jesus of Nazareth, the King of the Jews' (John 19:19).

When we come to look at the rulers (chapter 12 *John on the rulers*), we will find a group of people passionate about the writings they have inherited, who see their role as mediating the message of the writings to the ordinary people, which means that they also have an acute interest in understanding those writings.

One of the defining journeys in the nation of Israel's history, described in the book of Exodus, was the escape from Egypt through the Red Sea and on to Sinai where Moses received the Law and passed it on to the people. The Law, with the associated rituals, practices, feasts, fasts and worship, ushered in a special relationship with God. In time, the nation took this special relationship for granted, flirted with other deities and lost the plot so badly that in the end, as specified in the contract (Deuteronomy 28:15-68), it went into exile. That experience created a new commitment to engage with the book, to understand it, to interpret it and to live it out. After the exile, when a chastened minority returned, Ezra and the Levites who supported him, for instance, were interested not simply in reading scripture, but also in expounding it so that people would understand it (Nehemiah 8:7,8). The nation realised that deviating from the terms and conditions of scripture had led to serious trouble in the past, and it was determined not to make the same mistakes again.

Hence the focus on the writings. Jesus shocks this community in three ways. First, he claims that the writings they guard so assiduously are pointing directly to himself. The eternal life that the Pharisees, in particular, seek is not coded into the writings, but is available through the one the writings write about (John 5:39-40)! In the dynamic that emerges, this means that the Pharisees want to protect the faith against Jesus and his use of the writings, while Jesus tells them that they have grabbed this particular sword by the wrong end and are being cut to pieces by it. Their problem, Jesus explains, is not with him but with Moses (John 5:45). Moses is their accuser because they are not living out the righteous life that Moses wrote about, and secondly, Moses wrote about the one to come and Jesus claims to be that person. Moreover, Jesus claims to have the same authority as the writings – for instance, breaking the Sabbath at will (e.g. John 5:16-18; 9:16). So when the leaders meet someone who overreaches their authority, not just by questioning their grasp of the writings but by claiming the same authority as those writings, it is deeply disquieting. From their viewpoint, this threatens the entire nation (see, for instance, John 11:45-50).

## The Word that Argues Back

But the third shock is one that John introduced in the prologue with the section about the word becoming flesh (John 1:14). This isn't a message you can argue over, it is someone who will argue back.

Nobody who reads John's gospel can fail to notice how much of the narrative is taken up with talking – not just teaching the crowds or the disciples (although that is there), but the one-to-one interviews, the conversations with and about the people who have been healed, and especially the debates with the authorities. The whole structure of John's gospel would be so much simpler if there were not this on-going argument about who Jesus is and about what the writings say about him, the recurring debate that takes up so much space from John 5 to 12 and that breaks out again at Jesus' trial. Without these messy interludes, it would be so much easier to identify our seven signs and seven 'I am' sayings, and to make the clever connections that John has woven into the text. We, probably like the Pharisees, would find the narrative so much easier to follow if there weren't this cacophony of debate and dissent in between the elegant story-telling. But surely that is the point – the Word speaks into silence, into our searching and reflection, but also into daily activity, times of tension, and even above the noise of war.

Whether or not we fully understand all that is going on – and I admit I do not – we can at least recognise that the God who spoke over the darkness and chaos in Genesis speaks still into the anger, confusion, searching and explaining of humanity. And the Word has the same effect today in dividing society, the crowds, oligarchies, even the disciples, into those who want to silence him and those who want to listen forever.

We will return to this theme when we consider the interviews that Jesus had with individuals and the debates and discussions that took place with different groups in society, in chapters 10 – 14 of this book.

**The Last Word**

Although there is a note of ambiguity, John's narrative circles around the question of final judgement. Jesus claims that all judgement has been delegated by the Father to the Son (John 5:22), while at the same time asserting that the Son was not sent to condemn the world (John 3:17; 12:47), and that he does not judge anyone although his judgement is sound if he does (John 8:15-16). So does Jesus judge or not?

Maybe these verses help (John 12:47b-48):

> 'For I did not come to judge the world but to save the world. There is a judge for the one who rejects me and does not accept my words; the very word I have spoken will condemn them at the last day.'

I am not sure how you would make sense of this. Some might distinguish between Jesus as saviour during his life on earth and his return as judge, but however you read it, there is a clear reference to the final word of judgement.

And, as with the Pharisees, this picture of Jesus as judge is at odds with the narratives with which we are more comfortable – the Jesus who saves, who comforts, and who acts as our lawyer in the courts of heaven. We must return to this topic in chapter 3 (*John on the Spirit*).

**The Word of Power**

Sometimes I think fantasy and science fiction writers capture an idea that helps us with our theology – here it is, the idea of a powerful word. Today we might be more familiar with a key code that allows the Rebel Alliance to get past the Empire's guards not long before the famous discovery: 'It's a trap!' (I hope that hasn't spoiled *Return of the Jedi* for anyone.) Previous generations grew up with, 'Open Sesame!' Yet there is something more powerful here in John.

Years ago, when I was still reading to the boys most evenings (but when they were reading dozens, maybe hundreds of pages a week themselves), I came across Garth Nix's *Keys to the Kingdom* fantasy and read *Mister Monday*. I do not know what Garth's beliefs are, but his writing is laced with theological allusions, and each of the seven books in the series (named after the days of the week) focuses on one of the seven deadly sins. However, the bit that sticks with me is about the Will, which has been broken up and given to seven trustees who have each locked their piece away so as to prevent its fulfilment. The Will must be reassembled in order to be fulfilled and in each book in the series, another part of the will is released and the recovered pieces form more and more of the Will until it has all been recovered, when finally it has the power to change everything. And it does – not because someone enacts it, but because it has that power itself. This idea of sequences of words escaping and joining together in order to come into force was something I really enjoyed.

We are talking here about agency. We usually think of an agency as perhaps an office that helps us to plan our travel or an organisation that gathers intelligence for a government. However, we also talk about human agency – the way people make decisions and act on them to change the world around them – perhaps by farming the land or building cities. The thing that Garth Nix captures is the idea of words with agency, allied to great power.

If our concept of the Word is purely philosophical, objective, passive, or at the mercy of our interpretative abilities, we have missed the point. The Word is not simply the logic that lights up the reason of every human child. It is not written, as in Omar Khayyam's *Rubáiyát*, by a finger that moves on, leaving an ineradicable judgement. Yet neither is the Word something that we can continue to re-define over time, as we do with all other words. John's Word makes decisions, acts and reaches out to persuade, to argue, to convince and, if we will allow it, to save.

## Reflection

During the past couple of years I have been learning to compose and write music. I have enjoyed the education enormously and have gone about it idiosyncratically with spreadsheets and software, having never played an instrument in my life. Because I also like to write, I also produce most of the lyrics, which leads to an interesting question when things fail to fit – where does one begin the repair? In such circumstances, John, my music teacher, always alludes to the start of John's gospel and says, 'In the beginning was the word.' I think he says it with a small 'w' because he forces me to make the music fit the meter of the words, not to distort the natural flow of the words around a convenient metrical arrangement in the music. And in doing so, he has helped me to write better lines.

More profoundly, wonderfully, and with a transforming personal revelation, John starts his story in a similar place. He shows how we cannot fit the Word around the tune we were already playing, but offers something to those who listen and retune: 'those who hear will live' (John 5:25).

In this chapter, we have considered words as the cornerstone of communication and thought of the Word as someone sent. In turn, this led us to ask about other messengers and we considered the writings and the Word. The big difference is that John's Word comes in human form, not just as a messenger, but as the message itself. We glimpsed how shocking this was to the experts of the day and the tension it created between what they were expecting from the writings and what Jesus had to say. In a sense we are stretched by the same tensions – between what we think Jesus should be and what he wants of us. And finally, we have considered the power of the word in judgement and in making things happen.

These chapters are short and more focused on ideas than practice, so the questions provide a basis for reflecting on what you might do as well as on what you believe. So here they are.

## QUESTIONS

1 How might you prepare a short talk based on John's prologue, appealing to the theme of the Communicating Word, to introduce Jesus to a group of people who know very little about Christianity?

2 We think of communication in many contexts: through social sciences that we use to explore family relationships or organisations; in business, marketing, and advertising; as network technology and infrastructure that drives most modern life; as information theory, theories of knowledge and words; and in many other ways. Pick some aspect of communication that appeals to you and see how many modern ideas and metaphors fit with John's concept of the Word. What elements of our modern thinking do not really align? Why might that be?

3 Jesus tells his disciples that, just as he has been sent, he is sending them (John 20:21). As a follower or Jesus, think of three things you could do in the coming week to strengthen that reality in your own experience.

4 Your Muslim friends will see the succession of messengers, each delivering a divine revelation, in a different way to you because they see another prophet after Jesus. How does John's concept of the writings and the Word, of messengers and the message, address this issue? What kind of discussion might this help you to have?

5 Read 2 Corinthians 3:6. How does the contrast Paul draws between the dead letter and the life-giving Spirit influence your understanding of John's gospel? How does Paul's approach align with the ideas we have explored about the writings and the Word?

6 Matthew, Mark and Luke, the writers of the so-called 'synoptic' gospels, arrange their material quite differently to John. Give an example from each (preferably not an example that they all quote) that reports Jesus speaking with power? How does this influence your understanding of the Word in John?

7 Have you ever felt you were arguing with God? What happened at the time? What did you learn from it?

# 2 | John on… The Father

> I am ascending to my Father and your Father, to my God and your God. (John 20:17)

John is not unique in asserting the fatherhood of God – Matthew, Mark and Luke all report teaching by Jesus that draws the disciples in as children of God. Both versions of the Lord's Prayer begin, for instance, by addressing God as Father (Matthew 6:9; Luke 11:2) and the teaching on forgiveness (Matthew 6:14-15; Mark 11:26) and showing mercy (Luke 6:36) is couched in the context of our Father's reaction. But John is different.

I don't know whether you like word clouds – those brightly-coloured pictures where words appear in larger font because they have been used more often. For a long time I could not see the point of them, but these days I realise that they have their uses. Our final year students have to undertake a project in Computer Science or Business Computing and in our department we lay a lot of emphasis on creating an app, package or database that does something for a real person. To do that, you need to know what real people want. The students I supervise are almost always doing something in healthcare, so if you want to know what people want, a word cloud based on a hospital's website or patient blogs, or social media traffic about diabetes, for instance, gives you an idea of what the big issues are. Of course, just counting words is not enough, because people can use the same word in very different ways – but it is a start. After that you can begin asking about why the big words are there, and then you can build up a picture of what people are happy about and dissatisfied with. But it all starts by knowing what gets mentioned most.

Without building a word cloud, you can count occurrences in an English version of John very easily. If I search for the string, 'father', John has the most references (137 using my search engine and the English version of the gospels I have), with Matthew second (103) – although he uses 39 of those references in the genealogy at the very start of his gospel, which is a long list of human fathers. Luke is third with 56 and Mark has fewer than 20. However, as we have indicated, just counting is not enough, and many of the uses of the word 'father', especially in the synoptic gospels, refer to a normal father in real life or in a parable. There are some natural fathers and even forefathers in John, too, but the vast majority of references are to God as the Father. Beyond the numbers, John also has something special to say – what is it?

We have already thought about the sent-sending relationship between Jesus and his Father, so let's start there – why does the Father send Jesus? As far as I can see, there are two main reasons in John – the first is that nobody could know the Father unless he was revealed to people by the Son, and the second is to save the world.

## Knowing God

Very early on, John contrasts the ministry of Moses with the mission of Jesus (John 1:17-18) – Moses brings the Law, but grace, truth and the way to know the Father are through Jesus. Coming as it does at the end of his prologue, John is laying down an important marker here. He returns to this theme later as Jesus argues about Moses and Abraham with the adherents of one and the offspring of the other, a line of argument we have considered already.

So did the revelation that Moses brought misrepresent the God he went up the mountain to meet? Clearly, the aim of this book is to help you engage with John's gospel for yourself. So how do we feel around for clues without trying to define a full answer to a very tricky question? Well, perhaps I can begin by saying that I am not sure the question is a helpful approach. I think that understanding the difference between Jesus and Moses is more like grasping the difference between reading a biography about someone and meeting them in person.

The problem, says John at the end of his prologue, is that nobody has met the Father. So how do you find out what someone is really like if you cannot meet them and you have read all there is to read about them? One answer is to get to know their children. As humans, this line of argument is mixed up because genetics has a way of swishing the pool for every generation and nobody – at least yet – possesses exactly the same genetic fingerprint as one of their parents. However, it is not like that with God – Jesus claims to provide the true likeness.

Even so, we recognise traits that pass from generation to generation. Our youngest son has a distinctive walk, the same sort of walk as my wife, and indeed, as her brother. My wife is a practice nurse and someone came into the surgery one day and said that they had just seen her son and they knew it had to be her son because of the way he was striding along. I have worn artificial legs since I was three years old, so nobody walks like me, but on occasion I ask myself the question the other way around – how would the 'me' who had not required artificial legs have walked? Would it be possible one day to analyse the gait of each of our three sons, subtract the walking patterns of their mother, and work out how I would have walked? The 'me' without artificial legs is not accessible and cannot be watched, but I might be able to find out about that 'me' through my sons. It's not a question I am deeply committed to, but I do wonder every now and again.

Perhaps John is saying something like that here. Maybe John is saying that Moses tells us about what God does and expects – where God goes, if you like – but if you want to know how the Father walks, you have to watch how Jesus walks.

Because Jesus has come to reveal the Father, he faces the paradox that people would feel much happier if they could see the Father and assess the relationship for themselves. Even Philip says that a peek at the Father would be 'enough' (John 14:8-14). But that is the one thing that Jesus cannot do, because Father must be revealed. The crowd and the rulers have the same problem. On the one hand, the son of Joseph (John 6:42) cannot have come down from heaven. On the other hand, if he claims a different Father, where is that person (John 8:19)? Here we find Jesus at his most elusive. He argues that the Father testifies that he is who he says he is, but will not produce this most important of witnesses (John 8:12-30)! And yet at the end of this passage we read that many people believed. What is going on?

One of my favourite movies is *Star Trek IV: The Journey Home* – the one about saving the whales. I have never learned Klingon or had a cut-away drawing of the Enterprise on my wall, but I have watched too many of the original episodes and I like the humour of the film. I must say that my wife, Dani, does not really appreciate the original series (or any subsequent series), and will look up from her knitting to ask why Spock does not simply play his Vulcan harp to disperse the alien attackers who are hiding behind those polystyrene rocks!

Anyhow, *Start Trek IV* explores the relationship between Dr Gillian Taylor, custodian of two whales in a sea-life centre at Sausalito, and Kirk and Spock who turn up on her doorstep. One of the jokes is that while they have an immensely powerful spaceship at their disposal, it is temporarily incapacitated and as a result so are they. Gillian has to give the hapless pair lifts and to pay for her meal out with Kirk.

Yet Kirk intrigues her and she keeps wanting to know who he is. He is elusive, in a way that reminded me of John's narrative as I watched it again last autumn, about 35,000 feet up on my way to Australia. Because it is a film, we are in on the joke – Kirk and Spock are not idiots but they come from a different world and they cannot afford to attract too much attention because they have a job to do. Anyway, even if Dr Taylor is well disposed towards them, she is not going to believe the real story, nor do they know quite what she would do with the information, because she and they have very different plans for the whales. All of this makes Kirk cagey with his answers and I realise that I too would be cagey. Because it is a film and we can only enjoy the humour for so long, a time comes when the only

Californian from 1986 that they really care about discovers the space ship and the real capabilities of her companions… and everyone lives happily ever after in a very different world.

I catch something of a metaphor when I watch the film. The truth that John is telling us is much more disturbing than the scene everyone sees. It looks almost normal, but something odd seems to be happening. As viewers, we realise that it doesn't always even look normal, but we know that the reality behind the appearances is much wilder than anyone imagines. To carry the metaphor across, Jesus is careful because he has a job to finish and because, well, you can sense the exquisite balance of the situation, can't you?

**Invisible voice**

That is why the signs are so important (see chapter 5 *John on Signs*). Many people come to recognise that the signs could not be done, perhaps more importantly would not be done, unless God endorsed the Son who was doing them (John 14:11). That is why the voice from heaven matters (John 12:28-30) – there is another witness, but not one who can be forced to appear or to present evidence to any court of the day.

This is not simply an academic observation for John, however. This is difficult and dangerous territory, especially at the height of one such conflict (John 8:42-47) – it is not simply that they are worshipping God in an inappropriate way or that they have misunderstood something important about the God they worship. Jesus says that they have the devil as their father.

Most of us are much more comfortable with Isaiah's approach as he mocks the false gods, not because they are a real threat but because they do not exist at all. For Isaiah, God does not compete with other gods – it is not that there is a good God and other bad gods. For Isaiah, God is incomparable (Isaiah 40:25). There is God and the void. If you want to worship the void, says Isaiah, you are a fool. His analysis of idolatry is particularly ironic as he describes someone who takes a cedar bough and arbitrarily uses half as fuel to cook dinner and turns the other half into an object of worship (Isaiah 44:14-20).

So is John's world full of other gods again? Perhaps, but not necessarily. John's analysis is black and white – we revel in the light or creep into the darkness, we reflect truth or conceal error. For John, it is possible to think you are doing one thing but to be doing the exact opposite. In that case, what we think we are doing is only an illusion. So we cannot claim God as Father and have murder in mind (John 8:39-44). We cannot claim to be looking for God's approval if we really want the approval of those around us (John 12:43). We cannot fight for the truth with lies (John 8:55).

It is all rather distressing that such a crucial point should be so finely balanced, nor can we tell ahead of time how the worship story will work out. Many of the rulers cannot reach a point of belief and worship – although some do, including Nicodemus, Joseph of Arimathea (John 19:38-42) and a royal official (John 4:43-54). The woman at the well with the mixed-up spiritual heritage (John 4:4-42) gets there, as does the man born blind (John 9), although the chap who was healed after waiting by the pool for 38 years (John 5:1-15) does not seem to manage it.

So who are we worshipping and how do we know we are worshipping the Father?

## Nature and Nurture

Throughout John's gospel, Jesus' identification with the Father is completed. Having appealed to a genetic metaphor, we have the puzzling allusions Jesus makes to learned behaviour – he does what he sees (John 5:16-27). The Father is at work; the Son is at work. The Father raises the dead; the Son gives life.

I told a genetic story earlier about how my sons have inherited behaviour that I will never exhibit in the way I walk – but the opposite is also true. Our middle son told me that he didn't realise that scratching his chin with his upper arm was an odd habit until his friends pointed it out to him when he went to university. He realised that he was copying someone without elbows and he would not have learned that behaviour from any other father. So here is something else that is very surprising – the Son copies the Father. And as he copies, we learn.

## The Father is Busy

The story of the man born blind begins as the disciples try to work out who is to blame and as Jesus explains that the man is in this predicament as a visual aid to show off the good things that God does (John 9:3). Earlier on, and following another healing miracle, Jesus explains that his Father is 'always at his work' and that he himself is, too (John 5:17).

For most of us this comes as a surprise. Our prayers exhibit very little curiosity about what the Father is up to. If you listened to them you might conclude that there is not much for God to do apart from rescuing people from difficulties, some of which are quite trivial and many of which are of their own making. Maybe we have a view of a God who presides quietly above the hustle and bustle of the cosmos, a view which we probably do not adopt when thinking of any other head of state. In the real world, those heads seem to stay up late, get up early, and turn grey over disconcertingly short stays in office. As I write President Trump has just completed his first 100 days in office and his observation was that it was more difficult than he thought it was going to be – governing is a frantically busy affair.

So what is the Father busy with? To answer that, of course, you have to follow the Son. But, critically, John draws attention to the business of work and the importance of doing things. There is a question at the end to explore this further.

## What Is in the Heart of the Father?

Primarily, of course, the Father loves the Son (John 3:35). Throughout this gospel, that relationship sustains Jesus, directs Jesus, and gives him confidence in all he does – for he is not alone (John 16:32). The sense that this is a very old love is achingly evident in that last extended prayer that John overhears – or maybe it was meant to be listened to, I do not know (John 17). And the Father cares about the world. The most famous verse in the Bible (at least for an earlier generation) was one about the world (John 3:16). If you use Bible Hub, you will see that the word for 'world' gives us our word 'cosmos'.

Many years ago, the church where we worshipped was re-organising the children's groups, including those run during the morning service while the adults listened (or failed to listen) to the sermon. My wife came up with an acronym that stuck for many years: Club on Sunday Morning in Church: COSMIC!

And the Father has cosmic concerns, according to John. The world, the whole world, the groups who were expecting a Messiah (John 1:11), those who weren't, the global superpower represented by Pilate, and any powers beyond – God cares about them all. If you take a traditional line over authorship, then this is strikingly evident in the composition of the crowds in heaven (e.g. Revelation 5, especially 5:9) – all tribes, languages, peoples and nations – everyone!

The tension between love and care, between the Son and the cosmos, is central to the narrative – it demands elusive responses, it drives the timing and it illuminates the dark side of glory (chapter 7 *John on Glory*). Taking upon himself the coming cosmic destruction in order to save the world is the agonising sacrifice which, for the Son, remains both a choice and an obedient duty to the end (John 12:27-28). We will take these ideas further in chapter 14 (*John on the World*).

## Me Too?

It is very late on in the story – the evening before the night of trial – when Jesus springs a new truth on the disciples: the Father wants direct communication (John 16:23-28)! Up until that point, the disciples' personal relationship has been with Jesus, and now Jesus is saying that he will step back. They can approach the Father for themselves.

There is no *John on Prayer* chapter in this book – maybe there should be – but perhaps it would be like having a chapter on teaching children to talk in a book about parenting. Unless there is a developmental problem, my experience is that they learn to talk by themselves. And once they realise that your job as a parent is to feed, clothe, protect and entertain them – and that all of this can be managed through words – they soon master the brief. There are many good parenting chapters to be written on keeping up with all the questions, on when to say no, on when to answer questions and when to let them think a bit more for themselves, but you don't have to teach them to ask because they teach themselves and you are just the hapless assistant.

And so in a few verses, the secret is out! They can talk to the Father for themselves, and the Father is waiting to act on their behalf. This is the fulfilment of that part in the prologue about becoming children of God, not of 'natural descent' but 'of God' (John 1:12-13). That is what the perplexing talk with Nicodemus that night (John 3:1-21) was all about. Human beings can become children of God with all that such status entails. It means moving out of a place of judgement into a place of security (John 3:16-21; 15:7), it means seeing greater things (John 1: 50), it means doing greater things (John 14:12), it means, in our turn being sent as the Father's children to a deeply needy world (John 20:21).

So there is work for us to do. Denominationally, we tend to think of this work in different ways. At one end of the spectrum, we tend to be keen on evangelism, Bible translation, missionaries, Christian TV or radio. Others invest more heavily in social programmes, education, alleviation of poverty and providing someone to talk to. The idea that the Father is working and that for us, as it did for Jesus, every day brings at least one opportunity to do something that will bring glory to God – that is a challenge that John brings in his own special way.

The synoptic gospels are full of activity for disciples – especially in the parables – but in John's gospel we work because the Father is always at work.

## Reflection

Many of us would have kicked off a chapter on the Father by reflecting that the primary revelation John brings is of the Love of God. There is no *John on Love* chapter in this book – not because it isn't true, but because any short book on John will be dreadfully incomplete whatever it includes (and I am not the person to write a long book on John).

We have explored the theme of love, the love of the Father for the Son, and the way that people, people like us, can come to be included in that relationship. We have seen how Jesus develops the relationship with the disciples and then at the very end steps back in order that they can enjoy a more durable and ultimately dynamic relation with the Father. And then that dynamism sends us out to do good works.

Although this is hinted at, this story only becomes clear relatively late in the gospel. The earlier part concerns the arguments and debates about whether Jesus is really revealing the God whom his audience believes it is worshipping. As we observed, these passages are hard to follow – for me, anyway – and move into dangerous territory.

But finally for the true worshipper of the Father, there is a job to do, because the Father we worship is always busy.

# QUESTIONS

1 Use an online tool to see how many ways John 1:18 has been translated. Why do you think some translators use reproductive language (e.g. 'only begotten') and others avoid it? What truth is the verse expressing?

2 What is your favourite movie that shows you something important about the Father? Did the screenwriters and directors set out to illustrate this point, are you reading the message in afterwards, or is it simply in there because it is true and, as Francis Schaeffer used to say, all truth is God's truth?

3 What is the most cosmic aspect of your faith? How would anyone ever find out?

4 A friend of yours says that every faith is trying, one way or another, to reach the same God. Using John's arguments about lying and murder, how would you approach a discussion with that person?

5 How busy is the Father you worship and how is that reflected in your prayers? Try to remember things you have prayed about in the past week that recognise how busy the Father is and that respond with actions of your own.

6 Why was Jesus so upset about the trade taking place in his Father's house (John 2:12-17)? What would have to happen at your church for you to get as upset?

7 What sort of passion does John stir up in you about the Father? What are you going to do about it?

# 3 | JOHN ON... THE SPIRIT

> And with that he breathed on them and said, 'Receive the Holy Spirit.' (John 20:22)

As we saw in the last chapter, John has a habit of revealing things at the end of his gospel that we have not seen coming as we read through it. For instance, Jesus only expresses with complete clarity in the last hours of his life how much the Father wants the disciples to communicate directly and ask for things. Had we been listening to Matthew or Luke, we might have discovered this from the wording of the Lord's Prayer, but it comes as a surprise when John tells the story.

And so, when it comes to the Spirit, there is a bit of a bombshell at the end, for John concludes his narrative with a group of disciples in a locked room, receiving the Holy Spirit as Jesus breathes upon them. This leaves us with all kinds of puzzles – is John in conflict with the other writers, especially Luke, who has a very different narrative occurring several weeks later? What about Thomas who was not there – there is no record of a similar experience for him? Was Peter there, and if so, how can he be in on such a wonderful experience while there is still unfinished business in the final chapter – a sort of postscript to the gospel?

There are at least two paths into this question, each helpful in its own way. The first is that we will encounter in the next chapter (*John on Belief*) a similar pattern within John's own writing, where the disciples appear to reach a position of belief, but then we are told later that they believed at that point, and we are told later still that they believed because of something else that happened. So we have this pattern that something momentous happens and they believe but somehow they have yet more to believe. Unravelling that mystery is still ahead for us, but we can watch out for the pattern. And there is something, else, too.

## Centre of Gravity

I will watch almost any sport but I particularly like the mysterious something that happens in the high jump – as the athletes go over the bar, they twist, arch their backs and then flick their feet up at the last minute. The athletes – at least the winners – go over the bar, and there is usually a camera near the pole to allow you to watch them wriggle over. However, the remarkable thing is that their centre of gravity goes under the bar! I love that camera at the side and I always watch carefully in case, just once, I might catch sight of their centre of gravity sneaking under the bar while each bit of them goes over it.

It is magical – they only need enough energy as they push off from the ground to get their centre of gravity close to the bar, and yet every inch of their whole body passes over it. So what is really happening? Well, both are really happening – what we think of as being the essence of their physical dynamics, their centre of gravity, passes invisibly under the bar – while we watch their bodies pass over it!

I also get the sense that there is an invisible half to some of the situations John describes to us. When we come to study the disciples and whether they believe and what they believe when they believe, we like to put up a bar and measure their progress. When Jesus breathes on his disciples, we naturally want to compare it to a very different experience that Luke describes in Acts 2:1-4.

Since this seems to be a pattern that John is comfortable with – things repeating but not necessarily covering the same ground – maybe we have to leave this as a bit of puzzle. Maybe there is something going on that we cannot see, yet – an invisible piece of mystery.

So what is John saying? Well, we have noted how late in the day the revelation comes about the relationship the Father wants the disciples to enjoy. This is certainly true of the Word, whom they thought they had come to know, whom they thought they had completely misunderstood and in whom they come inexorably to trust. Perhaps the same is true of the Spirit. And as all these pieces of the puzzle come together towards the end of his gospel, it looks like John's narrative leaves the disciples with a much more integrated view of who God is and the relationship that they can enjoy, than is the case for any of the other writers.

However, doesn't this just take us back to the problem we are trying to puzzle out? Isn't John presenting a narrative that is incompatible with the synoptic narratives? Aren't John's disciples presented as being in possession of a revelation that their counterparts in Matthew, Mark or Luke are not? And I think the answer is, not necessarily!

## A Theology of Christmas

So let's ask a very different sort of question. When did you stop believing in Santa Claus? At first sight, this seems to be arguing in the wrong direction, from an innocent faith to a rather more cynical grasp of reality. But it is also a journey from partial knowledge to a fuller knowledge, and one in which you reached an integrated perspective on all you knew in a more consistent way.

For many people there was no single defining moment when they realised that the dolls' house had been put together by their dad, or the train set had been bought by their mum. Maybe they had had their suspicions for a long time but carried on with the strangely dualistic western Christmas theology about presents and mangers and shepherds and reindeer. My guess is that you started to sort this out quite early on, and when you found out all that was going on, it probably wasn't quite the surprise your parents – having forgotten their own childhoods – were expecting.

Children start out with a mythical present-giver and finish up recognising that they have known the present-givers all along. For them, the reality that they have a mum and dad is much more important than the myth of Santa Claus, even when they haven't sorted out all the details. Even when they don't have both parents, or are cared for by someone else, the reality of the person looking after them at Christmas is much more important than any number of songs about Santa and his sleigh. (I'm not complaining about the songs and play them in the car from as early in December as I can.)

As we read John, however, we are watching the disciples making a huge transition – not nearly as trivial as the one that I have just described, for my illustration is flawed in so many ways. They started out in search of a mythical person made up of all the good promises about the Messiah (whilst ignoring the sterner and more difficult prophecies), but they ended up with a working faith in the Father, the Spirit and the Word. John is not telling us that they have it all sorted out by the end of his gospel – the last stories he tells (John 21) explain how confused and unsure they remain – but he is saying that they have enough to continue their journey, enough to make sense of it all in the end, enough to live a believing life. Maybe John is helping us to see all they knew, even if they have not yet marshalled their knowledge into coherence, or enjoyed fully the life on offer to them – even if major revelations and experiences still lay ahead of them.

## Early Pointers

So what does John indicate early on that he will pull together toward the end? The first cluster of references (John 1:32-33) refers to the Spirit descending upon Jesus. The sight provided John the Baptist with evidence of who Jesus was, and it also provides a recollection that John the gospel-writer turns into a witness statement. It is peculiar that John does not know who the Messiah is, given the family connections (Luke 1:35-45) – but maybe here is another example of someone who had the parts of the puzzle, his suspicions, perhaps, but who had not put them together in realisation and revelation until he sees the Spirit coming down. And from the start, the Spirit points out who Jesus is.

The next clusters of references come in John 3 and 4 as Jesus talks first to Nicodemus and then to the woman at the well. In both cases, the reference to the Spirit stretches the discussion into a new dimension. In a discussion about new birth Jesus uses the phrase, 'born of the Spirit' (John 3:8) to drag Nicodemus away from a forensic analysis of faith. It's like human birth, says Jesus, but it's not just about starting over again. It is about starting in a new way. Starting again as a human will only lead to another grown-up human. So Jesus takes the reproduction argument – that you reproduce what you are – off in a direction that surprises Nicodemus. We are talking about… well what are we talking about? What is this dimension of Spirit?

When the one-to-one with the woman standing by the well at Sychar turns to the place of worship, Jesus wrenches the discussion away from our space and time with three uses of the same word, 'in', one for each of our spatial dimensions! Use an interlinear translation (perhaps Bible Hub) to pick up the repeated word: not on – 'in' – this mountain nor 'in' Jerusalem, but 'in spirit and truth' (John 4:21 and 23). For Nicodemus, the answer to the 'how' question is, 'born of the Spirit' (John 3:8) and for the woman from Sychar, the answer to the 'where' question is 'in spirit and truth' (John 4:23). Why? Presumably because 'God is spirit' (John 4:24). However, even here there is a degree of ambiguity, because some translations use a capital 'S' while others opt for the lower-case.

So, if the Word takes us back beyond the first creative command and forward past the last word of judgement, the Spirit takes us to somewhere completely new, where things happen, and can happen, in a completely different way. So what sort of completely different things does Jesus want his disciples to grasp before he leaves them?

## Life with a Capital 'L'

The earliest connection that Jesus offers to his disciples about the Spirit is the link to the new life on offer. We have already seen in the discussion with Nicodemus how the new birth is mediated by the Sprit. No Spirit, no new life – and this theme is rehearsed and repeated. Jesus associates the Spirit with the hard saying about eating his flesh and drinking his blood (John 6:53-65) – whoever consumes these will enjoy eternal life and be raised at the last day. However, and in almost the same breath, Jesus tells them that it is the Spirit who gives life. Later, when Jesus offers living water that will overflow from the individual into the world around, John adds two parenthetical comments: first, that Jesus was referring to the Spirit; and second, that the Spirit was still, in some way, to come (John 7:39).

So what is this life? There is no *John on Life* chapter, but if there were, we would have to explore two very different aspects to John's idea of life worth having. First there is eternal life – if you use an online tool, you will find five references in John 6. Interestingly, and closely associated with these, there are four references to being raised up at the 'last day.' Perhaps this is one of the reasons why Jesus' conflict with the Pharisees is so intense – they believe that there is a game to play for in the resurrection. There is no point arguing with the Sadducees, for instance, because they do not believe in this eternal dimension at all and so have no hope in that direction.

The second idea is of a life that is worth living now, guided, for instance, by the 'light of life' (John 8:12), a life, 'to the full' (John 10:10). And the Spirit is essential to both of these. But how?

It's a complicated sort of dance, as far as I can see, but John describes a process in which people come to the Word for life – Peter puts the case at its most plaintive, that there is nowhere else for them to go because Jesus has the 'words of eternal life' (John 6:68). However, no one can come to the Word unless the Father provides the ability to do so (John 6:65). If the Father draws people to the Word, Jesus goes on to explain that the Spirit prods them, convicting them of the things in their lives that need attention (John 16:5-11). Meanwhile, the Father and the Word have this life (John 5:26), while the Spirit brings it to us (John 6:63), and both the Father and the Word are credited in John with sending the Spirit (John 14:16-17; 15:26). So, does John present the Spirit as being in some way less than the Father or the Word, a sort of life-force that originates with the Father and the Son but is less than either?

This is very tricky territory, since we are touching on one of the most profound mysteries in the world (or out of it), but I don't think that John's picture locks us into that view and because of what else we know, I am sure that is not the case.

We have a similar question in nature, to which our understanding has changed radically in the past century or so. If you put a strong enough magnet under the table, you can pull the cutlery around, even though the magnet does not touch the knife or fork – and there are lots of fun videos out there to watch and learn from. We can describe what is happening in terms of fields that stretch out from the magnet and affect certain metals at a distance. So we have a view of matter – the things that are attracted to, or repelled from, each other – and the fields which carry the forces of attraction or repulsion.

In the past century, a new idea came along, which was that what we think of as force fields are simply particles zipping back and forth between other particles. If you think about two friends who each get into a coracle (a sort of dinghy dating back to the time of Julius Caesar) and spend an afternoon on a placid lake, and if you imagine that they take a ball with them and start playing catch, you have a glimpse of how these particle-forces work. As they throw the ball back and forth, their coracles will slowly move apart. If you imagined filming them from a drone way above the trees, you might miss the ball because it was so small, and just see two coracles drifting apart.

If you then shrink that picture down billions of times and speed it up billions of times, you get a glimpse of how we think about forces these days – particles attract and repel other particles by exchanging particles, it's all the same stuff. (You may have spotted that it must be more complicated than that because it is hard to think of a way of throwing a ball back and forth that would bring the coracles together and create an attractive force. To get there, you must grapple with some further unexpected weirdness in nature.)

Yet that is how we think that the world works, from inkjet printers to planetary motion (it still involves a degree of faith until some wrinkles have been ironed out about gravity). Maybe, in the shadowy world of quantum physics, we have a faint picture of what John is talking about: Father, Spirit, Word – all of the same – and yet being sent and exchanged. I don't know. If it helps, hang onto it. If it doesn't, ditch it.

## In Safe Hands

Because of this, a critical part of Jesus's work on earth is to effect an introduction between the disciples and the Spirit, just as he is working to introduce them to the Father. Perhaps not surprisingly, the two introductions reach a climax in the dialogue he has with them at what we think of as the Last Supper (John 13-16).

Jesus wants the disciples to know that they are not being left alone – they are being left in safe hands. Just as Jesus is not alone (John 8:16, 29; 16:32), they too will have company and support. I don't know how you read John 14:14-21, but clearly Jesus is addressing the sense of loss hanging over the disciples. They seem to know something is up, even if they are only sensing Jesus' own heaviness of soul and are responding with a sadness of their own. Whatever it is, Jesus promises that they will not be left as 'orphans.' Jesus says he will come to them and yet he is leaving them! How can both be true? The answer is that the Spirit is coming. So what is the minimum they need to know about the Spirit to survive when Jesus is gone?

## Continuity of Care

One of the big ideas in healthcare today is continuity of care – that the quality of the care you receive is not broken or downgraded as you move from specialist to specialist or from a clinic to a hospital, or from a hospital to home. Too often, there are problems with continuity of care – maybe you are a diabetic and you fall and break your hip and when you get into hospital, the management of your sugar levels goes out the window while they focus on fixing your leg. There are lots of small ways in which this can happen and the cumulative result can make hospital a very dangerous place for some people.

A few years ago, I took the train to York and a taxi on to the Royal Army Medical Corps to watch teams of doctors and nurses in their last phase of training before being sent to an army hospital in Afghanistan. They had put a lot of time and effort into making it realistic, with a scale model of the field hospital, and actors who were made up with lots of red stuff and even bits of silicone to look as though they had had limbs blown away. In the rehearsal these patients were brought through and the teams would have to process them, while assessors would wander around, scoring the teams for the job they were doing and especially on how well they were working as a team.

As I watched the process, there was one chap doing nothing – he had his arms folded but was keeping a careful eye on all that happened. I asked the expert next to me what was going on and he explained to me that this person did nothing himself, but was responsible for the patient's care in front of him. He would follow that patient all the way through the system, ordering up all the treatments of diagnostics. Being the army, they had an established hierarchy for orders and this chap's job was to ask the specialists what needed to be done and then order up what they recommended. Of course it meant that the patient received superb continuity of care – one person was there the whole time, looking after no one else!

That is the final piece of Jesus' revelation: the Spirit is coming to look after every aspect of their lives. Just as the Father sent the Son, so the Father is also sending the Spirit – 'another advocate' (John 14:15-17).

**Reflection**

When the first disciples first meet Jesus, they have no idea who he is, except that their Rabbi, John the Baptist, has seen the Spirit descend upon Jesus at baptism. At the end of the gospel, he breathes on them so that they, too, might receive that Spirit. Why? Because the Father knows that we need continuity of care – what the Word has started, the Spirit brings to glorious completion.

But what is it that the Holy Spirit does in us? Well, that they do not know – except that 'greater things' are in store (John 14:9-14)!

And now for some questions.

## QUESTIONS

1 How do you understand the relationship between the Father, the Spirit and the Word?

2 How do we see the Spirit in our world and what do we not see at all?

3 How does John explain what the Spirit does in the lives of people who are not yet disciples? How much of that can we see and how much can we not see?

4 Follow through the references connecting the Spirit with Truth – what is Jesus saying to the disciples there?

5 Use an online source or concordance to find the passages on the Spirit as advocate. Are there passages (perhaps beyond John's gospel) that identify Jesus as our advocate? What does this tell us?

6 Give three to four examples of how you have experienced the Spirit as your teacher? Have you any other aspects of care that you have experienced from the Spirit? Tell the story.

7 What are the 'greater things' (John 14:12) that Jesus had in mind? What has your experience of those been?

# 4 | JOHN ON... BELIEF

> What Jesus did here in Cana of Galilee was the first of the signs through which he revealed his glory; and his disciples believed in him. (John 2:11)

At the end of his gospel John explains that he has written so that people might believe in Jesus (John 20:31). But what is belief?

Is it about putting up your hand at an evangelistic event or going forward for counselling? If that sounds too easy, it is amazing how often it leads to a permanent commitment. Years ago, when we were studying Philippians at church, Betty made her way to the front and produced a little red book that had been given to her when she had responded at a gospel event. In the NIV, the verse inscribed in it reads, 'being confident of this, that he who began a good work in you will carry it on to completion until the day of Christ Jesus' (Philippians 1:6). Seventy years later, and she was still going strong!

Others cannot identify a single, life-changing, encounter. They have a faith but would be hard pressed to put their finger on a particular moment of decision or specific time of change. Indeed, people will have a range of experiences, some that embrace elements of the two possibilities just cited, and some that may be even more extreme than either.

So what is John's take? First, he talks a great deal about belief (see questions 1 and 2 at the end of this chapter). Second, he believes it is possible for anyone to come to faith. Finally, at least as I understand it, he has a surprising, multi-layered view of what happens when someone believes. However, the breath-taking basics are clear. First, belief in

Jesus creates a parent-child relationship between almighty God and ordinary people (John 1:12) and unlocks for us the relationship that he enjoys with his Father. Remember his words to Mary on that first Easter morning: 'I am ascending to my Father and your Father, to my God and your God' (John 20:17). Second, belief is the key to life (John 20:31) – life eternal (John 3:16, 36; 4:14, etc.), life to the full (John 10:10). Not that these are distinct themes, for they fuse from time-to-time – 'Just as the living Father sent me and I live because of the Father, so the one who feeds on me will live because of me' (John 6:57).

## Searching Questions

But we must press on. John asserts that belief transports us from a realm of judgement into new life. Although Jesus' hearers were deeply divided on the question of an afterlife, dying in their sins (John 8:24) was something they were desperate to avoid. So if there is a way to die with a clear conscience it is worth asking robust questions about it, especially if the stakes really are that high.

More personally, times come to most of us when our faith is challenged, when floods of doubt snuff out the joy and extinguish any sense of hope or purpose. The floods may be triggered by a loved one's death, difficult times, serious illness or even during professional success, but by then it is usually too late to focus on much beyond getting by from day-to-day. So we need to think through what belief means, now.

There are other valid reasons for taking a look at what happens when we believe, and they relate to baptism, to sharing our faith, and to running a church. For obvious reasons, most churches favour a formula for faith and if you are content and able to communicate within a framework of that sort, that is fine. My guess is that sooner or later you will need to think the topic through in a fresh way. So let's start!

## Seeing is Surprising

The Samaritan woman (John 4:1-42) and the man who was born blind (John 9) quickly lay hold of an effective faith that leads in turn to worship. Both have difficulties that would have been evident to themselves and to those around them – maybe the enforced transparency makes them such excellent communicators. In his case, the physical impairment of blindness was so inescapable that the chapter begins with a casual discussion, raised by the disciples, about whose sin led to the man's punishment – probably within earshot. Meanwhile, the woman's alienation from her neighbours leaves her to fetch her water at a most inconvenient time.

Strangely enough, there is a gateway through both barriers that opens up a one-to-one with Jesus. Other blind men had to yell above the crowd (e.g. Matthew 9:27-31; Mark 10:46-52) while other mums had to push hard for an audience (e.g. Mark 7:24-30), but these people are on their own when Jesus comes across them. Neither seems to have made the first move with Jesus but after that both show interest, then curiosity, and each finally realises that the person they have encountered is very unusual. The man who was blind demonstrates his faith in worship (John 9:38), while the woman's faith is evident by her witness to everyone else in the city (John 4:39).

So far we are in familiar territory when it comes to the journey of faith – approach, enquiry, dialogue, and public commitment.

## Two Steps Forward

More problematic are the disciples' journeys of faith. At least two had been looking for something before they met Jesus, since they were already disciples of John the Baptist (John 1:35-51). One is named as Andrew who goes to find his brother, Simon, who also becomes a follower of Jesus. We do not know who the other one was but since there are two prominent pairs of brothers who were close to Jesus, it may have been John who wrote the gospel, especially since he conceals his identity and disappears from view at every available opportunity. Or maybe it was Philip, since John continues the narrative with Philip (John 1:43) after he has tracked Andrew back to Peter.

Philip finds Nathaniel and we have an interesting exchange between Jesus and Nathaniel. As with the Samaritan woman, it seems to be the fact that Jesus knows something very personal about him that leads him to recognise Jesus as the Son of God and King of Israel, at which point Jesus comments upon Nathaniel's faith (John 1:50-51).

So what did these disciples believe? Three have committed themselves to following Jesus and one has made an amazing declaration of faith. It is a bit of a surprise then to discover that Jesus' disciples came to believe in him after seeing the miracle at the family wedding (John 2:11), and perhaps a bit more disturbing to discover later in the same chapter that it was after he rose from the dead that they believed the writings and Jesus' words (John 2:22). Nor does the pattern end there. On the first Easter, a disciple, presumably John, enters the tomb, sees and believes (John 20:8). A week or so later, Thomas reaches what sounds like a conclusive position of faith (John 20:28).

In between, we have intriguing references to the faith of the disciples. In the discourse that John relays from the upper room where Jesus and the disciples have gathered for their last meal, Jesus is still explaining things in order that when they come to pass, the disciples will believe – and it is still in the future (John 13:19; 14:29). Even at this late stage, Jesus is working on what the disciples believe and do not believe (John 14:9-11). It may sound a little harsh to us because he uses an argument he has used with the rulers – if you don't believe me, at least believe because of the miracles (compare John 10:37-38).

Although Peter has made a statement of faith that would satisfy most evangelical churches today (John 6:69) and appears to be representing the disciples as a whole when he does so, later on Jesus is glad that the disciples will witness Lazarus being called back to life – because it will help them believe (John 11:15).

So what is happening here? Do the disciples believe or not? Why, when they seem to have reached a position of belief, does Jesus think there is further to go and how can they come to believe all over again? Is this a spiritual game of snakes and ladders where you climb a ladder as you grasp something by faith but slip behind if you get swallowed by a snake?

It seems the most helpful approach to these questions is to ask what the disciples believed each time. John tells us what they believe. Like a playwright, connecting one scene to another, John presents a series of miraculous signs that Jesus performs, which we will explore in the next chapter. After the first of these, the water-to-wine sign (John 2:1-11), presumably the disciples believed that Jesus was the miracle-working Messiah. Did they believe he would rise from the dead? It doesn't look like they had really considered that. After the feeding of the 5,000 (John 6:1-15), when there was discord amongst his followers because Jesus had said people will have to eat and drink his body and blood, Peter asserts that they believe in him and are not about to desert him. On that first Easter, when the disciple who sprinted to the tomb finally decided to enter and sees the fabric lying there, what does he believe (John 20:3-9)? Presumably, he believes that Jesus is definitely not there and clearly something is beginning to dawn on him – but perhaps the full implication of what he sees is still not clear to him.

This paints a picture of a developing faith, that the disciples have a faith that encounters ever greater challenges until their expectations are trashed when their Messiah is executed and their shocked minds are blown away when he rises from the dead. Although their belief may be threatened by each more challenging problem, the end result is an even deeper faith.

## When Do You Have Enough Faith?

So, how much faith does it take to lay hold of eternal life or to become a child of God? If hearing and believing is the way that we cross to life from death (John 5:24), how do we know where the threshold is? How do we know where and when each of the disciples crossed it? How do we know if we have crossed it? Earlier generations put a lot of time into questions such as these.

There is a sense in which the threshold-crossing question makes me very uneasy. It sounds like something football fans or tennis players might ask when they want to know about goals or points – should we be looking for some celestial goal-line technology that tells us when someone has reached an effective faith? It does exist, but for some reason – and I can think of many good ones – we are denied access to it (2 Timothy 2:19).

One problem with asking this sort of question is that it does not really chime with the journey that the disciples took in coming to faith (nor, indeed, with that of Mary and Martha about whom there is a question at the end). A second problem is that it reflects a personal-achievement view of belief – because it makes it seem that getting over the line is all down to me. Jesus teaches that he gives his sheep eternal life and that no-one can release his grip on them (John 10:27-30) and it would be hard to think of a less achievement-oriented picture than that of a sheep caught in a tussle between the shepherd and the snatcher. But it explains why our evangelism produces more converts than disciples.

We do need to answer this question before we can work out how or when to baptise those disciples. In many parts of the world, baptism is so prejudicial to longevity that only an idiot would be baptised without really believing, but in the church where I worship and perhaps in your church, too, there is no such downside to sort out the real candidates.

If you baptise by immersion (my view, but I have friends who differ) you cannot do it in stages – an arm this week, a leg in a month's time – you must baptise the whole person. So how do you know if the whole person has a real faith, especially if faith flows and ebbs? Whatever your practice in baptism, it links critically to your understanding of belief, even when you baptise people ahead of a stage where they can believe for themselves.

So, what is belief and how do I know whether I am a believer?

## Barriers to Belief

Sometimes when I am stuck, I find it helpful to turn the question upside down. What about unbelief? Does John help us with that? It turns out that he does and has produced a lot of material on the subject. Those on-going arguments are full of what is preventing people from believing. So let's start there.

We saw in chapter 1 the sending-sent relationship between the Father and the Son. So the first barrier to faith is not believing that God sent Jesus. Appealing to one of John's letters (1 John 4:14), we have a central proposition: 'the Father has sent his Son to be the Saviour of the world.' For John's contemporaries, the Law of Moses – or rather their understanding of it – set the standard, and miracles performed on the Sabbath became the test case for them as they sought to categorise Jesus (e.g. John 5:8-16). They concluded he could not have been sent because he did not comply.

Whenever or wherever we live we carry cultural baggage, most of which we only become aware of as we encounter people from other places and generations. I am not sure it is any easier for people in our generation to believe that Jesus was sent – or any harder. If you are locked into a worldview where there is no God, then clearly the proposition is ruled out from the start. If you are already convinced that there must be multiple routes to God, then the proposition that Jesus is the only one sent in this way (John 14:6) will, again, not work for you – nor indeed if you follow a different prophet, line of prophets or philosophy.

We will return to this in the next chapter (*John on Signs*) and again in chapter 15 (*John on Evidence*), but much of the sporadic argument throughout the gospel is to find out whether there is an overlap of worldviews that will allow the crowd, the rulers, or anyone else, to accept the idea that Jesus is the sent one. Encouragingly, throughout John there is a steady stream of people from different walks of life who decide that the proposition is believable, and who come to believe (John 2:23; 4:41; 8:31; 10:42; 11:45; 12:42).

Similar arguments take place in our own day as we seek to establish a framework for a reasoned discussion about whether God could send his Son to save the world. Our challenge is less to understand the search for a shared framework in Jesus' day, and more to work out what it looks like in our day. Can we find places where this idea can be reasonably discussed with the atheist, the Buddhist, the Marxist, the Muslim, the New Ager, the occultist, or the pantheist, not to mention adherents to the many worldviews beyond and between those on this list?

## Beyond Assent

Yet even then we have not reached the sort of faith that John talks about. Mental assent is needed but it is not sufficient. There came a time when some people – John calls them disciples – who had followed Jesus decided that they had had enough (John 6:66). It sounds like they were offended by some of Jesus' teaching and stopped following. This introduces a further angle to John's idea on belief – it does not simply follow a line of argument, it follows Jesus. Jesus' last words to Peter are, 'You must follow me' (John 21:22), and it is as we follow that whatever has happened, mysterious and privately inside, becomes obvious to all.

Just as we think we are clear about belief that starts with a proposition – that the Father sent Jesus to save us – and that we step out to follow him, Jesus introduces the shepherd in John 10. The sheep follow, not out of intellectual commitment, nor indeed following any decision – they follow the voice they recognise (John 10:27-28). So there is also something instinctive about faith that develops a sense of where the shepherd is and decides to go there, too.

Finally, with his homily on the vine (John 15:1-17), John returns to the agricultural metaphors that so richly adorn the other gospels. To the astonished apostles in Luke 17:5-6, who ask for an injection of faith, Jesus reminds them that the mustard seed, which is incredibly tiny and looks nothing like the full-grown plant, has a capacity to grow and develop out of all recognition. Seeds have all the coding needed to adapt to their environment, whether they simply and naturally fill a forest or move concrete as they grow. There is a sense that the disciples do not know what they believe, but they believe enough to discover more later, and there is a hint of this when Jesus is washing Peter's feet (John 13:7).

## The Relationship

So then, mental assent, commitment, something innate and instinctive – those are the ingredients – what is the recipe?

In July 1998, I stood next to Dani who was wearing an amazing dress she made herself, before a congregation, where we both made promises to one another. It wasn't difficult since by then we had done the thinking and had started to make other commitments, not least the mortgage going through. It was also fun, a day when Dani looked stunning and every joke was laughed at, a day we thoroughly enjoyed with family and so many friends.

We have, of course, learned a lot since that first public commitment to be man and wife and stick together until death us do part – so much we did not know when we started out. There are also things that I knew then that I don't know now. I used to know a great deal about how to bring up a family and now I don't. I am surprised that God has been so good to us and it has all turned out so well.

But you realise as you look back that the only thing that remains is the memories and the relationships. The houses come and go, as do the computers and the cars, the clothes and even the toys. We are still in touch with well over half of the people from that day who are still alive, and we have new roles and relationships as a result – mum, dad, grandpa and nanna. The sense of being together is the most wonderful part, that life is an adventure to navigate as a pair. Our main discovery has been of the goodness of God in guiding us through it all.

Clearly the relationships have flowed from that day of commitment, but relationship also drew us to it. I think that John's take on belief in Jesus is a bit like that.

## Drawing It Together

John is clearly passionate that people should come to believe in Jesus. He presents example after example of people who do come to believe and detailed argument after argument with people who, on the whole, do not. Although the pattern varies, there are recurring themes – encounter, interest, engagement, and a decision to follow.

John believes that anyone can come to believe and uses metaphors that are utterly obvious and also mysterious, such as shepherds and their sheep or a father and his children. Meanwhile, in watching those who have crossed over into belief, John describes a process which is not simply onwards and upwards, but he describes a quality of belief that develops, and develops out of all recognition from where it started.

John's narrative challenges us to find the ways in which the basic Christian premise – that God sent Jesus to save the world – can be understood and discussed in a rational way with those around us. It challenges us especially about our relationship as we follow.

## QUESTIONS

1 Use the string (sequence of lettets), 'belie' to search through the English text of John. This will take you to all of the following words in John: 'belief', 'believe', 'believed', 'believes' and 'believers'. What does this tell us about John's interest in believing? What do you make of the fact that there are no hits for 'belief' in John? What online sources can you find to help understand the words John uses (e.g. http://catholic-resources.org/John/Themes-Believe.htm [date accessed 17.4.17])? How can you use such resources to enrich your Bible study and ministry?

2 What was the royal official (John 4:43-54) looking for? How about the man by the pool (John 5:1-15)? How would you describe their journeys to faith (or not)?

3 How does John narrate the developing story of Mary's faith and that of Martha? What did they believe at the start of John 11? How about when Jesus first arrives? And by the end of the chapter? To what extent does this mirror your own experience of faith?

4 'Do you now believe?' By John 16:31, what have the disciples grasped and how is their faith about to be challenged?

5 What have you learned about baptism from considering John's take on belief? Do you baptise people in good time, too early or too late in your church? What is your reasoning?

6 Do you think John would seek to classify the person who believes in the proposition that Jesus was sent to save us, but does not follow Jesus in any observable way? If so, how?

7 To what extent are we tempted to record what we can observe, rather than to wait for the fruit of faith to become unmissable?

# 5 | JOHN ON... SIGNS

'Unless you people see signs and wonders,' Jesus told him, 'you will never believe.' (John 4:48)

A striking feature of John's gospel is the miracles he relates, the way he calls them signs, and the way he numbers them, leading us to expect a sequence – maybe there will be seven! Also, most signs are followed by a discussion, so there is a pattern there, which leads us to ask, what signal lies behind the signs?

## The First Sign

John tells us that Jesus' first miraculous sign took place in Cana, where Jesus turned water into wine (John 2:1-11), and it seems a flawed choice at first. How can we have any confidence in anyone who planned this wedding? If the families are unable to organise a drinking session at a wedding – and our own idioms of incompetence revolve around a similar scenario – how can we rely on anything they have a hand in? If they miscalculated so badly with the guest list or the wine merchant, who is to say that they might not have discovered a few more jars about the place at the crucial moment? In the general confusion, who's counting anyway?

As it happens, precision is unnecessary. The six stone jars of water needed to turn the tide (John 2:6) contain 500 litres, maybe half as much again. The problem was not to be resolved by discovering a couple more wineskins at the back of a cupboard.

Also, someone *is* counting – Jesus' mother (John 2:3). Running out of wine was a social disaster of such proportions that the family would be unlikely to escape the stigma for at least a generation. So, is this a disaster-recovery story, which meets our expectations of a miracle, or an insider/outsider story where the insiders are worried to death – which we might expect of a sign? In a sense, it is both.

The servants know what has happened (John 2:9). Indeed, the genuineness of the narrative is best attested by the absence of song and dance (so to speak) about the sign itself. The sign was to protect the happy couple from notoriety and it does just that, even if that is not really what we think signage is all about. The servants know, the women relatives know, at least one of the disciples knows, but they value the good name of the host too highly to say much. I like to think that the couple were in their graves before John spilled the beans, but who knows.

One other person knows something is up, and it is his job to stay sober and on top of things. The 'master of the banquet' is perplexed – why has so superior a wine been introduced so late in the proceedings (John 2:8-10)? He had assumed that the bridegroom would follow tradition and kick off with the best he had. This new vintage has him stumped – why waste it on a crowd whose palates have been dulled by days of partying? We are not told how far he pressed the point, or whether he followed his nose to the answer, but his wry observation is evidence that something remarkable has taken place. Does it convince you? If so, of what? If not, what would it have taken to convince you had you been there? John leaves it with us and moves on, with a reference to glory, to which we must return (chapter 7, *John on Glory*).

## All in the Timing

John's second signpost points to a royal official's son (John 4:46-54) and again, it looks like an odd choice. The son has a desperate fever, the son recovers. In terms of fever-healings Mark has a better story about Peter's mother-in-law who recovers so dramatically that she rises from the couch and gets straight back to her normal routine (Mark 1:29-31). This two-hander is an elegant puzzle in which the solution only becomes clear as everyone sits down and puts it all together afterwards. The mystery is that father and son are so far apart, so that it is only afterwards that the father realises that the time ties up – not to the second, since sundials and fevers are not amenable to such precision – but to the hour when Jesus told him that his son would recover.

Coming on the tail of our last chapter (*John on Belief*), we must ask if it convinces you. You could argue that the son would have recovered anyway, and I don't suppose John would stop you. But the timing will still bug you. There is a story about a man who got lost in a forest. Later, he was explaining to his friends in the pub that he had become so desperate that he had prayed out loud and asked God to rescue him. Well, his friends wanted to know, did it work? Oh no, he went on to tell them, before God had a chance to do anything, a passing hunter had shown him the way home.

I don't remember this next story because I was very young at the time, but I had a serious spell of malaria in the Middle East and a very high fever, while the anti-malarial drugs my Mom had were not working. Did God answer the prayers of my missionary parents? Well, an American doctor was passing through and took charge, and I'm still around. On its own, it is hardly evidence. But as part of a pattern, such events catch our attention – just as it is the bigger pattern to which John keeps signalling.

## If You Say So

The next miracle is the healing of the disabled man by the pool of Bethesda one Sabbath (John 5:2-15), and although John does not refer to it as a sign, most of us are counting, and we expect to get to seven. John seems to be more interested in the story because it signals a change in the weather – curiosity and mild cynicism are giving way to opposition, particularly amongst the intelligentsia.

Certainly, the man himself is a reluctant witness – the years of waiting by the pool have attenuated his expectations to the point where he cannot believe anything good will happen to him and his reaction afterwards is underwhelming, especially in view of the energetic behaviour of others who were similarly healed (e.g. Acts 3:1-10). The key point about this miracle – and the critical evidence – comes from those who catch him wandering around with his mat under his arm. There would have been no problem had he been lying quietly on it next to the pool, and he would hardly have been conspicuous had he carried it on any other day. As we have already observed, it is all in the timing – this was the Sabbath. The timing means that this man is easily picked out and interrogated. The irony is that he only gets into hot water because he was healed in the first place, and like the previous sign, it has to be pieced together afterwards, at least by those seeking to make a case against Jesus.

So far, John has provided three miracles, none of them furnishing the sort of in-your-face evidence we might have expected of something that John wants to call a sign. John has time, of course, and some of the later signs are truly spectacular, but for the present he is still building his case. The brush stokes are subtle but they are well placed. So, how does the emerging picture look to you?

There is something else here, for John is not simply recording evidence for a numerate generation, two millennia down the line, who have some grasp of science. He is introducing his friend and saviour. A second type of question to which we must return, then, is what do these signs tell us about Jesus? What kind of a person would help people out so effectively and yet try to avoid the limelight? What sort of person could do these things just by speaking?

## Filling the Void

The feeding miracle (John 6:1-13) is a heartening one for any parent of growing boys who need a gazillion calories a day. In terms of a theoretical framework, boys accept the notion that three square meals are good for them and reject the dogma that heavy snacking is bad. With practice, any growing boy can interleave the two very satisfactorily. Unfortunately, they grow so fast that anxious parents soon develop a crick in their necks when delivering the healthy eating lecture.

While the crowd is so absorbed with the teaching that it forgets to make provision, it is a boy who has his next meal lined up. John is careful to note what has been counted – loaves, fish (John 6:9) and baskets (John 6:13) – and what has not been counted – the people (John 6:10) – but that is not really the issue here. As with the wine, it is the scale of provision that makes the impact. No-one denies that a miracle has taken place and most are more concerned with how or whether this connects with the provision of manna in the desert that God had made through Moses.

When some of the crowd find Jesus the next day, he answers them, 'I tell you the truth, you are looking for me, not because you saw miraculous signs but because you ate the loaves and had your fill' (John 6:26). So even then the emphasis is on the fact that they have been satisfied, rather than that a miracle has taken place. What do you make of that? As for those who were there first time around, they began to form clear opinions about Jesus (John 6:14): 'After the people saw the miraculous sign that Jesus did, they began to say, "Surely this is the Prophet who is to come into the world."'

## Wind and Water

John's next miracle – or is it a pair? – receives more extended coverage in Matthew (John 6:16-21; Matthew 14:22-34). Here, Jesus sends the disciples off while he has some down time, presumably in prayer, and then walks across the lake to meet them. The miracle of Jesus' walking on the water is briefly described, while the way in which they reached their destination 'immediately' (John 6:21) is mentioned almost in passing. However, there is mastery in the subtlety of the painting of the scene, while John's estimate of how far they had rowed in the storm and his record of the disciples' terror (John 6:19) on encountering Jesus unexpectedly both ring true. Then there is the corroboration of the crowd, as it counts the boats – discovering but a single boat missing – and yet finds Jesus on the other side of the lake. But what do you make of it all?

## Still in the Dark?

The preamble to the next miraculous sign indicates that John has several reasons for relating the story (John 9:1-4). This one is my favourite, perhaps because so many aspects of the evidence are critically explored, but probably because it is hard not to like the man born blind or to admire his guts.

First, then, there is some doubt as to whether this is really the same man who used to beg, or whether this is a doppelganger (John 9:8,9). The look-alike asserts that he really is the same man, and sticks to his story under severe pressure. There is also the problem that, at first, the man cannot identify the person who healed him (John 9:12), but since Jesus has been active once again on the Sabbath, it does not take the Pharisees long to solve the puzzle. Helpfully, they do not believe that this man was born blind and fetch his parents to confirm his identity. The parents are terrified of the risk of excommunication, and so their testimony is brief (John 9:20-23) but it removes any doubt as to their son's identity. Whether they believe his story or not, the Pharisees are left with two uncomfortable end-points – which becomes a feature of John's narrative around signs as we move later into his gospel. The man started out blind but he can see by the time the Pharisees interrogate him – they cannot challenge the former and there is no sense pretending he cannot see now.

It is worth asking why the Pharisees were naturally sceptical of this miracle. It was not because they did not believe in miracles. In fact, of the two major groups in the ruling council, the Pharisees were the more open to the supernatural. You may remember that Paul decides to split the Sanhedrin when on trial himself, with a declaration about his belief in the resurrection (Acts 23:1-10). In that narrative, Luke helps us with an explanation, 'The Sadducees say that there is no resurrection, and that there are neither angels nor spirits, but the Pharisees acknowledge them all' (Acts 23:8).

Their problem, as John points out, is that this miracle runs counter to their understanding of God's revealed purpose. 'Some of the Pharisees said, "This man is not from God, for he does not keep the

Sabbath'" (John 9:16). Their worldview was based around a revelation from God, validated and proven over more than a millennium. Their very existence as a nation was evidence that God did not change his mind, and that he kept his promises over many centuries. Their confidence in that worldview was not to be shaken by a miracle or two. To help follow up this important point, there are a couple of questions at the end. However, in terms of the flow, we note from here on an increasing hostility on the part of the authorities towards Jesus and an indifference to the message of the miracles.

## Wake Up Call

If you have been counting, we are up to number seven when Jesus calls Lazarus back to life (John 11:1-44), and for some that will be significant. Jesus' own resurrection is clearly a sign, but not in the way that he has been performing signs for or on behalf of others up to now. Jesus' own resurrection is in a different class entirely from anything else John relates, except perhaps the incarnation. So this is the last of the signs, and indeed, the rest of the gospel concentrates on very different material (except that John decides to write a postscript and relates perhaps the most extreme was-it-an-all-in-the-timing-or-not sign). But I will leave the counting challenge to you and your favourite commentary or online resource.

As with the blind man, but with even more care, John establishes the end points – that Lazarus was dead before Jesus yells into the tomb, and that he was alive afterwards. I guess this way of stripping the problem to its basics, of standing back far enough that you focus only on the starting and finishing points, appeals very much to me. As a discipline, physics teaches you the benefits of being able to stand back from the detail. Plans for perpetual motion machines are a good example: the more you are drawn into the detail, the easier it is to be persuaded that all the forces will always swing round and drive the wheel forever. However, if you stand back, you realise that energy is being dissipated, typically as noise and heat through the bearings, and that the energy has to come from somewhere. So unless your perpetual motion machine is secretly connected to a generator, it will slow to a standstill in the end. Perpetual motion machines do not work, a conclusion that is often obscured if you dive into the detail.

John is good at standing back. The passage of time from when he was part of these events until he finally commits them to writing creates a perspective from which standing back is quite natural. As usual, it turns out to be a little easier to establish that Lazarus was alive at the end of the story than it is to prove that he was dead at the start. John reports on a feast afterwards that Lazarus attended, along with others who came out of curiosity to see what a raised-up man looked like (John 12:2, 9). He also reports – perhaps tongue in cheek – on a plot by the chief priests to assassinate Lazarus (John 12:10).

That Lazarus was dead is ensured by Jesus' delay in setting out for Bethany at the start of the story (John 11:6). Jesus waits two more days after the sisters' message reaches him and, on arrival, discovers that Lazarus has been in the tomb for four days. Each sister, Martha and then Mary, declares her take on the situation 'if... my brother would not have died' (John 11:21, 32). Their friends and neighbours weep freely because they know he is dead (John 11:33). In the shortest verse in our English Bible, Jesus is caught up in these waves of emotion and also weeps (John 11:35), while no-one doubts the state of the decomposing body (John 11:39).

However, John also wants us to understand that the resurrection was clearly in response to Jesus' call (John 11:43), even if there is very little to describe. There is the prayer beforehand and then that magnificent yell into the dark – and out comes Lazarus. Again, it provides some of the onlookers with enough evidence to put their faith in Jesus (John 11:45) and precipitates a crisis meeting of the Sanhedrin. 'Here is this man performing many miraculous signs. If we let him go on like this, everyone will believe in him' (John 11:47b-48a).

## PS

The last miracle that John records (John 21:1-12) comes as a postscript, and in many ways it draws together everything John has been saying throughout his narrative. The disciples are back on the lake and getting nothing from the water. A stranger yells to them that there are fish on the right side of the boat, and suddenly they are overwhelmed with a haul, but the net does not break. They recognise the stranger standing by a fire with fish and bread as Jesus — he invites them to add their catch to the barbecue and join him for breakfast.

We are back with a sort of nature miracle, where the water behaves unexpectedly — we are back to subtlety, to eating and feasting, and back to the timing. There is a sense of newness that makes us think it is all starting over again and, indeed, the story takes off in a different and unexpected direction. If it is like what used to happen, it is also new, for this is a very private miracle, one shared amongst friends and written up as a bit of a secret sign, rather than one for public consumption. It is an enigmatic story as only John can do enigma — why do the disciples not recognise Jesus, why is the air so full of unvoiced questions again, why is it a bit like it was at the last supper (John 16:17-19; 21:12)?

## Reflection

As we stand back from these stories, we recognise that they furnish some of the evidence that John has assembled, that he is convinced will compel others to believe in Jesus.

But it is not simply evidence or facts: John believes he is revealing something personal. In these signs, we see connections to Moses and God's provision in the Old Testament, we are drawn to the heart of the Father, averting disaster for an unfortunate couple, we meet a master over nature, undoing death and disability, and filling the hungry. We catch sight now and then of a sense of elegance — the stories that can only be pieced together afterwards — and even of something elusive that we puzzle over, still. There is a personality behind the performance and John is keen that we should meet him. That is all he ever wanted.

As we noted in the last chapter (*John on Belief*), John is interested not just in our being convinced, but also in our being committed to follow. The signs in John have this same dual sense of purpose. Had they been solely about evidence, half of them would not have been reported, since they were not observed by the masses – indeed, one of them could not have been observed at all, since it occurred in two separate places. But if we think about them in terms of who Jesus is as well as what he can do, we may be more satisfied in our reading.

We will return to the question of evidence later (chapter 15, *John on Evidence*), but first some questions!

# QUESTIONS

1 Following a television documentary on Jesus, one of your neighbours wants to know more and has invited you around tomorrow afternoon. He tells you that his grandson has been studying the miracles of Jesus at school and you decide to prepare by looking at the signs in John. Which one would you choose and how would you structure two or three themes to pass on to your neighbour?

2 Which of John's signs do you find the easiest and which the most difficult to believe? Why? Which is your favourite and why?

3 Take your favourite miracle from John and list all the things you learn about Jesus from it – don't be afraid to spend a few days mulling it over. What have you discovered as a result?

4 How many of John's signs would have reminded the people who first saw them of something that Moses did?

5 List the people who did not immediately recognise Jesus after his resurrection? Why do you think this was? Is this evidence in favour, or against John's assertions?

6 Why is there often a discussion associated with each of the signs? If John is out to do more than establish facts, how could you focus on one of his signs in order to develop a deeper sense of worship?

7 Do any of the signs help you to think about more effective ways to witness?

# 6 | JOHN ON… I AM

'Very truly I tell you,' Jesus answered, 'before Abraham was born, I am!' (John 8:58)

This verse brings together two constructions that appear throughout the gospels but which are especially associated with John's writing. 'Truly, truly' is a formula that Jesus uses to underline what he is about to say. The 'I am' statements come in different forms and say something emphatic. We are not going to pursue the former in a chapter of its own – I have to leave you some fun things to follow-up yourselves – but we will look at some of the 'I am' statements.

This is technical territory and most commentaries will provide some insight and the internet is also full of material. When we spent some time last summer at church looking at the times where Jesus says, 'I am', I had not been browsing long before I came across a Roman Catholic resource, (http://catholic-resources.org/John/Themes-IAM.htm) put together by Rev Dr Felix Just, a Jesuit scholar and Executive Director at Loyola Institute for Spirituality in California. I know nothing about the chap, but I like his material because it is clear – perhaps a bit too much of a list for some – and there is plenty of it. I have used his lists in gathering the ideas in this chapter together. In fact, the repository contains much on John – or *The Fourth Gospel,* in his terminology – including an analysis of the 'Truly, truly,' sayings. So, if you can spend a bit of time nosing about the area and finding a source that you like and can get something from, you will be richly rewarded.

## A Burning Statement

In the Authorised Version, our banner text is even more dramatic: 'Before Abraham was, I am'. The imagination of the original audience would have been captured by this, too, because the words connected to an electric event in their history. In their collective mind's eye, they would have seen an old man in a desert, but it wasn't Abraham. Indeed, it would not have been the old man who drew their attention, but the bush before which he was kneeling and the voice he heard.

The story (Exodus 3:1-17) was etched deeply into the national memory, for this was the commissioning of the great prophet, Moses, when God appears to Moses as an unquenchable bush fire that refuses to consume the bush as fuel. Instead of flaring up and dying out it continues to burn, so much so that Moses wanders over to see what is happening, at which point a voice speaks from the flame, and the rest is history – Moses leads the Children of Israel out of slavery into nationhood and gives them the Law of God. Centuries later, the poets cannot get over the marvel that God should let people know through the Law what was expected of them (Psalm 147:19-20).

As Moses receives his mission and instructions in front of the flaming bush, the first of many concerns that are racing around his head emerges as a question. How is God to be known – what is his name (Exodus 3:13)? Again, there are all kinds of meaning wrapped up in the word, '*name*', and later in the same passage, Moses is given a different formula that is more familiar to us – the God of Abraham, Isaac and Jacob (Exodus 3:16). But the exceptional revelation that Moses receives here is to refer to God as 'I am' (Exodus 3:14). Even with this level of explanation, we have dodged around some really interesting teaching and truth, so there is plenty to go looking for (see question 1 at the end).

All of this would have connected itself together in a flash in the minds of the those hearing this rabbi make that same claim, even though it was in a different language and era. That is the odd thing about this passage – he is not just claiming to have pre-existed Abraham (although that is in there) – rather, he is claiming to have spoken from the bush, or at least to be equal to the voice that spoke that day.

Almost every step that Moses took in leading the Israelites from slavery to the threshold of the promised land involved a degree of divine intervention – food, water and protection from their enemies. However, it was especially in introducing the nation to its God that Moses' ministry was remembered – the Law, the place of worship, the priesthood and the glory of the presence of God that glowed at night and stood over the camp by day (Exodus 13:21-22).

This is the cultural backdrop to John's gospel (John 1:17), and much of the material we are about to explore makes connections directly to experiences the Israelites encountered with Moses. It is a key that unlocks John's thinking and indicates how the Word relates to the writings as well as to several of the other signs, while helping us to see why Jesus is drawing parallels between himself and Moses. On several occasions, the 'I am' is as stark, although the context is softer: to the woman by the well at Sychar (John 4:26); to the disciples on the lake (John 6:20); twice more in the argument leading up to our banner text (John 8:24 and 28); in the discourse to his disciples on that last evening (John 13:19); and finally, during his arrest (John 18:5, 6 and 8). Even over the distance of time and across the separation of language, this revelation carries a sense of wonder and a tingle of excitement.

This statement conveys God's relentless restlessness, over the years and across the centuries, to be with us: wherever and whenever we need to be rescued.

To Moses with his unreasonable mission, there is the reassurance, 'I am.' To the disciples in the storm, comes the cry, 'I am!' For the woman by the well there is an answer, not specifically to the questions she was asking, but to all the unasked questions, too: 'I am!'

The sense of timelessness in the present tense used is not simply a rhetorical device: it means that the same thing applies today, thousands of years after Moses and even the events John describes in his gospel. The impact of this truth is to offer rescue against insurmountable odds, to provide comfort in the face of impossible heartache, to forgive despite the claims of an implacable avenger. Wherever, whenever, however we got there.

In threading this theme through his gospel, John aligns the message that Jesus brings with the revelation captured by the greatest writers of Scripture – Moses, the psalmists, the prophets – and through the personal context, he establishes that Jesus is not claiming, as we noted in chapter 1, to be a messenger. He is claiming to be the author of the message, setting himself not beside these prophets, but beside the one whose message they proclaimed. John makes the final connection with these 'I am' statements, that Jesus, as the Word, is the message, too. For many of those first listeners, this claim ignited the blue touch-paper and exploded the debate.

### Is That All?

For most of us, these references, stirring as they are, are not what we think of when we talk about the 'I am' statements – we tend to think of the words, 'I am' followed by something –bread from heaven (John 6:41), perhaps, the door (John 10:9), the shepherd (John 10:11), or the vine (John 15:1). We feel there should be seven of these, and it is certainly possible to find seven, but it may help to reflect a little before rushing in to count.

My first reason for caution is that Jesus refines and sometimes repeats the same statement, maybe in a slightly different way, so we have to be clear what we are counting. In John 6, for instance – after feeding the 5,000 – Jesus says, 'I am the bread of life.' (John 6:35) He repeats the same claim (John 6:48) but there are also two variants: the 'bread that came down from heaven' (John 6:41) and the 'living bread that came down from heaven' (John 6:51). So is this one statement about bread in fact two statements (one about bread that gives life and one about bread that is alive), or even three (the added bit about coming down)? The same problem occurs when we come to look at the good shepherd and the door. Clearly there are connections within these groups of sayings, but we must be careful about how we group them.

The collection of sayings about bread is anchored deeply in the story of a miracle (see chapter 5, *John on Signs*) in which a crowd is fed, and the discussion that follows it. Some of the crowd who were fed cross the lake in search of Jesus and when they find him, they want him to give them a sign, rather as Moses did when the Israelites were fed and watered in the desert (Exodus 16 and 17). I cannot understand why they want another sign, but it sets the scene for the first part of the discussion, which is about the manna that God gave the Israelites through Moses (16:4-32). As we have noted, we are expecting John to be making these connections. Jesus' first intervention is to explain that Moses did not produce this nutrition (it came from the Father) and he goes on to describe 'the bread of God' that 'comes down from heaven and gives life to the world' (John 6:31-33) – although he does not use our special clause.

Thus, a pattern emerges in which something that goes back to Moses is replicated in some way by Jesus, a debate ensues, and the episode is sealed with one or more 'I am' statements. Moses triggered the bread supply that fed a nation, but Jesus claims actually to be the bread that gives life.

## Making Sense of It All

In the story of Moses, the water of life (Exodus 17:1-7) follows a chapter after the bread of life (Exodus 16), and John follows up with a water story (John 7:37-39), but the fluid piece in this debate is about eating flesh and drinking blood (John 6:53). So how do we take in this teaching, today?

Many years ago Dr Ivan Lowe and his wife Margaret, together with their two small daughters, left the groves of academia for the jungles of South America to reduce to writing a language spoken by fewer than 100,000 people – the Nambiguara tribe. I met the family when they had broken the back of the job and gone a long way towards translating the New Testament into Nambiguara, when Ivan was a linguistic consultant to others setting out to provide written translations in other boutique languages. We still communicate at Christmas, although Ivan and Margaret are well and truly retired.

Translation forces you to wrestle with a passage until you really understand it, and Ivan used a section of John 6 to describe how difficult it is to capture meaning. The first problem is that bread is not the staple in South America that it was in the Middle East two millennia back – instead people eat manioc. However, is living manioc the same as living bread? Well, the next problem was that living manioc already has a meaning – it is raw manioc. This does not leave us with a very inspiring 'I am' statement. Ivan read us a back-translated version of the final Nambiguara passage – it was considerably longer than the text we have in English, but it succeeded in using a relevant metaphor and infusing it with the sense of how Jesus brings life to the world.

This passage and others like it – especially relating to the Last Supper – have been subject to a debate over the centuries between Catholic and Protestant churches. In particular, views diverge over the way in which we consume the body and blood of Jesus and receive life by doing so. I am not planning to rehash those arguments, largely because I don't think they make as much sense today to either side, nor to the general public. Abstract and existential thought has so permeated our worldview that we can see these as metaphors that can also be true. Nor are we (yet) sufficiently consumerist as to believe we can eat or drink our way to heaven. Yet people – on either side of the divide – have lost their lives because of the way they understood passages such as this.

## Let There Be Light

I will leave it to you to work through some of the other 'I am' sayings and to connect many of them back to Moses. You might like, for instance, to connect the light of the world (John 8:12) to the guiding, fiery pillar in the desert (e.g. Exodus 13:20-21). John has prepared us for the light-of-the-world connection in his introduction (John 1:4) and so the link with Moses goes back beyond the illumination in the desert to those first spoken words of Genesis.

Some churches have light parties at the end of October as an alternative to celebrating Halloween, but it appears that we are a couple of millennia late with the idea because the Feast of Tabernacles (which is where we are in John 7 and 8) links its water-drawing event to a night – perhaps nights – of wild torch-wielding and dancing beneath giant lamps. Carson provides the background in his commentary.

Putting all of this together helps to understand how cleverly John has arranged his material from John 6 to 8.

## Metaphorically Speaking

John's gospel is beginning to swing in a different way around our banner text in the sense that, up to this point, the metaphors have been relatively concrete – bread, door, light, etc. From here on, they are much less tangible – resurrection, life, truth. It is not a categorical watershed; since there is the passage on the vine (John 15:1-8), and you might even argue that 'the way' (John 14:6) conveys a concrete rather than an abstract picture. However, something is changing as we move into the second half of John.

There is a sense of majestic urgency when Martha tells Jesus that she knows her brother will rise again, and Jesus says, 'I am the resurrection' (John 11:21-26). This is not a claim for the classroom, or something to reflect on in difficult times. This is a cry of victory from the edge of disaster. Even two millennia later, it forces us to move our evaluation of Jesus up or down and our view cannot remain where it was before we heard it. The primal cry to Lazarus later on is the answering echo to this claim that Jesus makes.

Again, there is plenty for you to follow up on your own when you consider these second-half 'I am' statements, and I trust you have a joyous time in that pursuit, but they do illustrate the difficulty of classifying the sequence. Where does 'I am the life' fit in? Does it go on its own, as part of the resurrection statement (John 11:25), or does it go with the way and the truth (John 14:6)?

## The Gate

As we have already noted, the 'I am' statements of John come in slightly different forms – the bread of life, the bread that came down, and so forth.

Our last example comes after our banner text but is very tangible – the gate or door (John 10:7, 9) and its connection to the good shepherd (John 10:11, 14). One of the great benefits of living in the internet age is the wealth of videos that explain, in just a minute or two, something profound in the text. Nosing around last year for material on this passage, I found an American pastor, Jay McCarl, giving an al fresco exposition of the passage (try: 'Jay McCarl door of the sheep'). As well as providing a visual explanation of sheepfolds, he shows how the shepherd(s) would literally become the gate to the fold by camping in the gap overnight. And these insights are just a few clicks away, cut into bite-sized pieces and ready for us to devour. What a privileged society we are!

So how many 'I am' statements are there in John 10? I don't know, but once you see the connection between the Good Shepherd and the gate, it doesn't really matter. The rest of the teaching in John 10 that wraps around these startling claims – one flock, one shepherd (John 10:16) and one gate – prepare us for the more exclusive version in John 14:6 – no other way to the Father!

## By Torchlight

We thought earlier about exuberant dancing in firelight, and there is one last torch-lit scene towards the end of John's gospel. It is another sacred time and the choreography is carefully managed so that the main performers can avoid making themselves ritually unclean. The mood is not one of celebration, however, but it is here that we see the impact of one of those great 'I am' statements, more clearly than anywhere else. It is repeated three times in the narrative to great effect (John 18:5, 6, 8) although our modern translations tend to add 'he' after each, 'I am'.

In an unintended piece of footwork, the soldiers and the officials with them react by drawing back and falling over the first time Jesus says, 'I am'. The physicality of their reaction tells us what a forceful message Jesus has conveyed – so if we cannot hear how important this is for ourselves, John is keen that we should observe its effect.

## Review

The number of times that Jesus says, 'I am…' and the ways in which he follows it up is a special feature of John's gospel. We have seen that these statements can be linked together – a string of pearls, maybe – where each draws us in and where together they have something bright and mysterious to offer. However, we can also see that they are usually couched in something else that John is presenting – maybe the statement goes with a sign, or is the conclusion to a particularly difficult debate. Taking each one in that context opens up a new view of what John is revealing about Jesus.

Finally, we see that in the first half of his gospel John is establishing a relationship between Jesus and Moses – the relationship we have already seen between the Word and the writings. We have noted the way in which the phrase, 'I am', would have reminded people of something unutterably ancient and holy, but John is not seeking to put Jesus on the same level as Moses – shocking as that would have been to his audience. So what is he saying? We have seen how some of the signs mirror signs that Moses gave, but the narrative this time is different – Jesus presents himself as the substance of the sign, not merely the channel through which the blessing flows.

In the second half of his gospel, John presents Jesus as someone given to the most amazing claims about himself, calling Lazarus back to life or telling his disciples at the Last Supper that he was the one and only way to the Father.

Got all that? Then how about some questions?

## QUESTIONS

1 The name we have as *Jehovah* or in more modern settings, *Yahweh,* uses four Hebrew letters, the nearest of which for us are YHWH. Apparently, this is closely related to the 'I am' clause. What do Exodus 3:14, Deuteronomy 32:39, and Isaiah 48:12; 51:12 tell us about God's self-disclosure to people? In what ways have you sensed the mystery or power of Jesus as 'I am' this week?

21 Why do you think the soldiers and officials fell back when Jesus says, 'I am' at his arrest (John 18:2-11)? What was Moses' reaction to the burning bush (Exodus 3:1-4:17) and are there any links between the soldiers and Moses in their reactions?

3 Look at stories in which Jesus and Moses are discussed together. How do the other gospel-writers present Jesus as being fundamentally different? How does John take a fresh approach.

4 Spend a little time looking at the 'I am' statements that are followed by 'the...' and see how many ways there are to group them. What do the different ways of grouping them teach you about Jesus? What is the most helpful part of the exercise?

5 Why do you think there is no 'I am' statement that relates to the water of life? Using passages from John 4 and 7, explain the links that John wishes to make about water, life and the Spirit.

6 What is the context in which to understand Jesus' saying, 'I am the light of the world' (John 8:12)? Use a commentary or go online to work out whether it is the festival reported in John 7, the incident with the woman caught in adultery (John 8:1-11), or the argument that develops into John 8. It may take a little research, but what do you come up with? What has drawn you to that conclusion? How do you now understand the saying?

7 CS Lewis (search online and read some of his books, if you haven't done so already) developed an argument in which he said we were forced to one of three conclusions about Jesus – either he was mad, bad, or God. What does John's sequence of 'I am' statements contribute to this analysis? How helpful do you find this?

# 7 | JOHN ON… GLORY

My Father, whom you claim as your God, is the one who glorifies me. (John 8:54)

GK Chesterton said that if a thing was worth doing, it was worth doing badly, and church banners may bear him out. While some are creatively designed and skilfully produced, many bear a different hallmark. However, even a basic construction can deliver something profound and memorable. I recall a simple banner which said, 'GLORY to GOD.' The word 'GOD' appeared in a bright circle, with the word 'to' above the circle, and above that, like the roof on a house, the letters of the word, 'GLORY,' with the 'O' at the apex. As I looked at it, I noticed that this arrangement placed the letters 'L' and 'R' from 'GLORY' at the same level, the 'L' on the left and the 'R' on the right. This banner rescued me on more than one occasion from whatever was supposed to be going on, as soon as it occurred to me that there is a left-handed and a right-handed side to glory, with John. In fact, I think this two-sided idea about glory is very helpful in unlocking his views on the subject.

At one level, John's idea of glory is something that we can all identify with – glory consists of amazing things that happen – a blind man, for instance, who sees everyone and everything in dazzling colour for the first time. Let us think of this as the 'right' side of glory, not in the sense that it is correct, but because it is probably the side that most appeals to us and that we can identify most readily in a passage. It is also the sort of glory we tend most readily to identify with.

There is, however, a glory for John that goes with suffering, where Jesus recognises, for instance, the humiliation and pain of his death and yet embraces it as part of glory. This is a sterner sort of glory, not one that we generally aspire to experience. It is hard to grasp what John has to say about glory without thinking of this other – left-handed, if you like – glory.

This is not simply a distinction based on brightness, to which we turn next (chapter 8, *John on Light and Darkness*), since some of the most uplifting glory occurs in the gloom, while some of the most painful is on display in broad daylight. I hope, then, that if we can keep our eyes open for shining glory and for sterner glory it will help us move in John.

## Eternal Light

Most of us are really only aware of the 'right' side of glory, the unbearable brightness of the presence of God. We remember Moses' special request to soak his soul in the glory of God, and how his wish is granted in part as he stands in a crack in the rock (Exodus 33:18-23). Or again, when he comes down the mountain with the Ten Commandments recorded in stone for a second time (Exodus 34), with a radiant face so frightening that he has to cover up whenever he addressed the nation. So, does brightness equal glory?

In dedicating the temple, Solomon paints in deeper colours: 'The LORD has said that he would dwell in a dark cloud' (1 Kings 8:12; 2 Chronicles 6:1). An aged friend of mine, who had little time for lengthy public praying, used to take great delight in pointing out that this prayer can be read in about seven minutes, even though it is the longest in scripture. At the end of Solomon's prayer there is glory, the sheer pressure of which excludes even the priests from the new temple (2 Chronicles 7:1-3). Does darkness equate to mystery?

## Glimpses of Glory

Isaiah, with his visions of glory and his messages to an obstinate nation, Ezekiel and a dozen others, had also contributed to the concept of glory shared by the community about which John wrote. Near the end of his prologue, John adds a personal note: 'The Word became flesh and made his dwelling among us. We have seen his glory' (John 1:14). There has already been the gleam we associate with glory in the references to the light that shines and enlightens. Already John is starting to weave together threads such as light and life as only he can, and it seems there is even a reference to Moses – Bible Hub will help you identify the camping word John uses as he explains that the Word came to live among us. He sees the same sort of temporary accommodation that Moses introduced and recalls the glory that filled it from time-to-time, perhaps also the fiery pillar that illuminated it from above.

While glory for John is something he has seen and experienced, there something subdued and underplayed about it, too. It is a glory from within, and from within a particular person, rather than a blinding glory that bursts out. From the start, John underlines this glory of character by linking it with grace and truth (John 1:17). Underplayed, too, at Cana with the miracle that most people do not even find out about (John 2:1-11). No flash or bang in the gloom of the kitchen or catering tent, maybe during the evening, but something changed profoundly before the contents of those jars were poured out. There is also something profound for the disciples as they catch a glimpse of glory (John 2:11). So, is this not what we would expect?

Indeed it is, and there is more. The blindness of the man in John 9 is not down to him nor to his parents, but provides an opportunity to see God at work in his life (John 9:3), so the irony of the leaders trying to force this man to back down and encouraging him to 'give glory to God' is not lost on John (John 9:24). Even Lazarus' death is for the glory of God (John 11:4) because of the resurrection.

## A Darker Glory

Amid the accusations and argument, the idea of glory surfaces again (John 8:50, 54). Passages such as John 8 and John 12 should be read with Isaiah's prophecy in mind. As the communication breaks down, to the anger of the audience and the frustration of the preacher, the link is not lost on John, who quotes Isaiah and ties the quotation directly to the theme of glory (John 12:37-41).

> 'He has blinded their eyes
>> And hardened their hearts,
> So they can neither see with their eyes
>> nor understand with their hearts,
>> Nor turn – and I would heal them.'
> (John 12:40; compare Isaiah 6:10)

In fact, John goes further and asserts that Isaiah saw Jesus' glory! The scene from which the quotation comes is another commissioning event, this time in Isaiah's vision in which he volunteers to go as God's prophet, and receives the rather downbeat encouragement.

So where is the glory? It is sprinkled throughout these passages but not in an uplifting way. How can there be any real sense of glory in the accusation that Jesus is just out to glorify himself? In John 11 and 12, several streams of activity reach a climax. The entry into Jerusalem before a jubilant crowd represents a high point in terms of public approval, while the opposition of the religious rulers hardens as they realise that their strategy is going nowhere (John 12:19). John has suspended his series of signs – is he finished with glory, too?

In a busy, crowd-filled day, some Greek converts to Judaism who are attending the festival want an audience with Jesus. They cannot, or they do not presume to, approach Jesus directly and so they approach Philip who goes with Andrew to see Jesus. Jesus' response is perplexing (John 12:23-29). It starts as we might expect, 'The hour has come for the Son of Man to be glorified.' But before long he is into seeds that die in the ground, about letting go of our lives to hold on to them forever, about following and being honoured by the Father. Then instead of seeking an escape from the crisis, he embraces it with the cry (John 12:27), 'Father, glorify your name!'

Jesus has already linked the desirable with the repugnant when he was teaching about the 'bread of life' (John 6:43-59) and where he sustains a metaphor that is both wonderful and appalling, depending upon how you listen. But what is Jesus saying as he nears this glorious climax, now that there is something frightening and horrible about it, as well as deeply attractive? When he first talks about being 'lifted up' (John 3:13-15), Nicodemus hears a positive a reference to a snake on a pole that brought recovery (Numbers 21:4-9). But it is a two-edged symbol. In John 8:28 and now here (John 12:32-33), we know that the phrase refers to his crucifixion – a humiliating and torturous execution. It embraces both exaltation and execution. What sort of glory is that?

Is the suffering itself glorious? The difficulty with making the connection that way is that it focuses on the suffering as a good thing and may even breed a sort of spiritual masochism, which hits the pain and misses any gain. Peter recognises that it does not take any special skill to suffer – murderers and other criminals, even meddlers, routinely suffer for their art. The redeeming element in suffering is that it be 'as a Christian' (1 Peter 4:12-19).

The question for us is: how? John provides us with some metaphors that may help. In this passage, we have an agricultural illustration (John 12:23-26) where the seed planted dies and multiplies. No death, says Jesus, no harvest. A second image is of a mother in childbirth where the pain precedes great joy (John 16: 20-22). When our eldest was born, my wife Dani lined a Moses basket, knitted a blanket and several outfits and photographed him in the basket, surrounded by needlework and clothed in wool. In the album, she has written under the photo – 'All my own work.' Out of agony came achievement – a sentiment of satisfaction recorded by Isaiah's servant after the 'suffering of his soul' (Isaiah 53:11).

So it seems that John has this view of glory – the deep colours and the bright colours are bound tightly together and cannot readily be teased apart.

## The Voice of Many Waters

Given his interest in glory, it is surprising that John does not provide a transfiguration narrative or that the only angels in the gospel are a pair whom Mary finds inside the vacated tomb (John 20:11-13). If his colours are muted, however, his soundtrack is full of surprise, pace and excitement, reminding us again and again of breath-taking events just out of our sight. There is the voice of John the Baptist, declaring that he has seen the Spirit descending upon Jesus (John 1:32-34). There is Jesus with a voice that will wake the dead (John 5:25), crying out to the living (John 7:37), and as predicted, to the dead (John 11:43). There is the spectacular rumble after Jesus calls out, 'Father, glorify your name!' The crowd hears thunder, but John makes out the words: 'I have glorified it and will glorify it again' (John 12:27-29). No lightning, but an awe-inspiring voice-over.

To the end of his days, John is alive to the glory of the voice. It is a trumpet-like voice that sounds of rushing water, which attracts his attention on Patmos (Rev 1:10-16).

Living under one of Heathrow's flight paths reminds us every day that louder does not always mean more powerful. Since Concorde's demise, the loudest (and most magnificent) of visitors has been silenced for good, so these days if you hear an ear-splitting crackle it is almost certainly 30 or 40 years old with fewer than 120 passengers. Meanwhile, the superjumbos whisper their way into the air. John is like that, leaving us a restrained rumble that takes away one's breath, or breathes fresh life in. Until the resurrection itself, the story of Lazarus is the most shocking and tangible evidence of glory. A dead man is a living man once more. It does not take strobes, spotlights, or a fanfare for us to understand the spectacular implications of all of this.

## From Glory to Glory

When I first turned my hand to writing this chapter a dozen years or so ago, I had just spent a couple of weeks watching the world's best athletes competing in Helsinki. I am a vaguely informed couch potato who was cheered, for instance, to have recognised Ed Moses when he joined the team in the studio for one of the finals. I love the last few laps of those long distance races where a runner or two will take off and sail effortlessly away from the field. I love it so much that I am even prepared to endure most of those early laps, where nothing happens at all, and I only occasionally lapse into a spot of channel-surfing in search of action.

I have enjoyed too much of this long weekend on the internet, nosing around to see what actually happened that summer. However, from what I can make out, 2005 was not a stellar year for British athletics, so there was a little more pressure on the relay teams as the championships wound to their conclusion. As recently as the previous year, a men's team had struck gold at the Olympics in Athens, so there was more pressure on them.

We tend to like sports that we do well in and although I don't think there has been a British 100m world record-holder since McDonald Bailey in 1951, we do sporadically well on the track, with two golden Olympians in the men's event – Alan Wells in the '80s and Linford Christie in the '90s. However, we seem to be good at relays, which are only partly about having the fastest sprinter in the world. Most track events are for individual glory – Paula Radcliffe had ground the opposition into her marathon dust and duly enjoyed her spot on the podium. With the relay it is all about getting the baton around: not everyone has to be good out of the blocks, but you do have to take care with the baton. Every year some highly fancied team manages to fumble the handover, or run out of the box – and 2005 was no exception. The baton changes the dynamic and creates new opportunities for glory.

As we move to John 17 and that great prayer that Jesus prays, the concept of glory shares something with a relay race where the baton is passed from hand to hand – sometimes in pain and distress, sometimes in elation: but it comes home at last. It came home for the British in 2005 with a pair of bronzes, the men in the 4x100m and the women in the 4x400m.

The theme of passing glory – not fading but being passed from one to another – has already been developing in the lead-up to this great prayer. Jesus has already explained to his disciples how they can bring glory to the Father through fruitful lives (John 15:8). In this prayer the glory glows brightest at the start and near the end of the prayer. At the start of the prayer there is a personal sense of climax as Jesus nears the end of his run. There was glory before and there will be glory again (John 17:1-5), even if the final strides will be laced with pain.

I guess the nearest I have ever come to that sort of gasping expectation was when swimming a length underwater – those last few strokes when you want to breathe and mustn't and you want to reach the end and then do. You end up taking pseudo breaths when your lungs want to go in and out, but you won't let anything in, before, finally you take in that first joyful, refreshing lungful. As you are gasping in desperation and the glow of achievement, perhaps you have captured in a very faint way the feelings of endurance and expectation that animate the glory throughout this chapter.

At the end of the prayer, however, there is a handover of glory, passed to his disciples; indeed, the next laps are already in view when others will believe as the disciples' take their message out (John 17:20), and suddenly we catch sense the cataract of glory cascading from generation to generation, going on and on and on.

## The Rainbow through the Rain

This sustained, final agricultural, metaphor of the vine and the fruit maintains the emphasis on our need to connect the left and right sides of glory in our everyday lives. The fruit is clearly the 'right' side of glory, but a darker glory goes with pruning that leads to fruit (John 15:1-8) and in one of those accidents of numbers, the same verses in Ezekiel's prophecy (Ezekiel 15:1-8) provide a helpful backdrop to this passage. Ezekiel dwells on the insignificance of the vine as wood, with the tacit acknowledgement that the value is all in the fruit, whereas John's passage contrasts the fruit with the pruning.

These transitional passages call us not just to observe the glory or to enjoy what we see, but to embrace it, whether by the choices we make or even in the times when we cannot escape it. Just as John believes that anyone can believe, so he believes that anyone can participate in the glory – real glory, passed down glory, passed on glory, left sided glory as well as right sided glory.

The idea that we, too, can participate is underlined in two further passages. After the resurrection Jesus commissions his disciples, sending them as he has been sent (John 20:21,22). More obliquely, the final reference in his gospel to glory relates again to death, but this time, not to the death of Jesus, but to Peter's death (John 21:19). The glory, shining and stern, is moving on.

## Reflection

There is an unnerving edge to John's idea of glory. As John writes, the theme of glory burns brightly in the past and will blaze again in future, but in the present, in Jesus' present, and in the present each of us faces, there is also a sombre side to glory – a left-hand side as well as a right-hand side to it.

As John watches Jesus, he sees glory in the things nobody else could do, in the grace extended to all, and through the truth unflaggingly unfurled. He watches people walk again, see again and live again. He hears the writings interpreted with a skill and passion he has never heard before. Throughout it all he hears voices raised in praise of God. I think that is the glory he refers to in is prologue, the glory of grace and of truth (John 1:14).

That is not all he sees, for he weaves in darker colours another side to glory that almost repels at times. He watches and sees that Jesus does not shrink from this sterner glory but that he reaches out to embrace it. At times it seems that Jesus is not even aware of the danger, like a toddler reaching out to grab a sparkler, but in the end that explanation will not do: Jesus understands all about glory and dives ultimately into the darkest mystery of all, returning to tell us that it is OK.

From there John leaves us to work out our response, to move from the stands to the track, to shed our scarves and overcoats, to find the baton and to pass it on.

## QUESTIONS

1 What glory stories in Exodus, Leviticus, Numbers and Deuteronomy may have influenced John's writing on glory? What allusions does he make directly or indirectly? You may have to use some online sources to find these connections and to think them through.

2 Read Isaiah chapters 6 and 53. In what ways do you think Isaiah's writing has influenced John?

3 For those who have studied the War Poets (and there is plenty online for those who have not) what connection do they make between death and glory? What other war poetry can you think of that contrasts with their views? Is any of this relevant to John's take on glory?

4 What connections do films about war make between death and glory. What films have something to say that might chime with John's approach?

5 To what extent have the two sides to glory been linked in your life and experience? What elements of John's glory do you feel you have already experienced or seen at first hand? What choices might we make with our time and money that would draw us into a deeper experience of glory?

6 John's view of glory delivers us from the question, 'Why me?' when we encounter bad times. How can a godly understanding of suffering help us to make the most of difficult times?

7 From John's other writings – especially in Revelation – how has Jesus prayer in John 17 been fulfilled. What is Jesus doing in glory now?

# 8 | JOHN ON... LIGHT AND DARKNESS

I am the light of the world. Whoever follows me will never walk in the darkness but will have the light of life. (John 8:12)

Rowan Williams, in his Holy Week reflections (*Christ on Trial*), notes the cinematic qualities of Mark's writing, cutting rapidly from scene to scene under a spare voiceover, with a pacey narrative full of action and drama. If Mark is the film director, John is the street photographer, choosing each scene and its lighting with care, from his first allusion to primal darkness to his depictions of that Easter dawn, when Mary Magdalene sets out, 'while it was still dark' (John 20:1). Not long before that, Judas had slipped away from the upper room: 'And it was night' (John 13:30).

Light, darkness, and shaded textures form the backdrop to the narrative and conversations. Sometimes the darkness provides a framework in which the light shines brighter. Elsewhere the time of day sets a sympathetic ambience for the events described – John is aware of the illumination and takes care to ensure that the story complements, or contrasts with, the lighting.

The twin themes of light and darkness are perhaps the easiest way to engage with John's gospel, attracting our attention or piquing our imagination and they lie close enough to the surface for us to discover them for ourselves. Remember, Christmas provides an annual opportunity to talk about these themes and the motivation to meditate upon them. So let's take it from there.

Mark dives straight into his gospel but the others each provide an introductory gleam in the darkness. Matthew has a star that shines in skies darker than ours, unpolluted by our light of night, and hints at the royal splendour of Matthew's King (try Colin Nicholl's *The Great Christmas Comet*). Luke builds his scene with care, to a soundtrack of hymns ancient and brand new, following Mary and Joseph through a swift and cruel dusk and ending in the hopeless acceptance of a lean-to for the night. Soon, an angel bursts upon a group of night watchmen, scattering the darkness with a blaze of glory and a grand burst of choral music.

Nothing less for John, although he paints on a broader canvas. In a phrase that takes us back to the start of Genesis, John retreats into the very beginning. I understand that in the original his prologue shimmers lyrically between poetry and prose, but even in translation its cadences and repetitions reach out and inspire us. Maybe we get more from it than earlier generations, with our existential heritage and Big Bang theory to cheer on that first flash of creative light.

## Out of the Dark

From the start, John is making connections – the light and the witness, for instance. I had always assumed that Mark starts with John the Baptist because he is so keen to get on with the story, but John is not under the same pressure and yet he does the same thing – he cannot allude to the darkness or describe the light without a witness. Clearly John the Baptist is a much more important character than many of us allow. However, John is also emphasising the visibility of the light – you cannot have a witness if there is nothing to see.

Then again, why should the light require a witness? Surely a light in the dark, a light before which the darkness must inevitably retreat, is self-evident! The trouble is, John does not believe that everybody will naturally, or of their own accord, recognise the light (John 1:10,11).

If we think that light implies something obvious, then we may have missed John's intent. Even this, one of his boldest images, is carefully nuanced. Evident? Certainly. Unmissable? In a sense, yes. Compelling? For John, yes, and he hopes so for us, too. But you can avoid it, if you want. You can look the other way. In chapter 9, John provides us with a delicately blended story of a man who cannot even see the sun as he sets out that day, but when it dawns upon him who Jesus is, he worships. Woven into the same story are a group of people who can see perfectly well, physically and educationally, and yet they cannot, for the life of them, share the blind man's perspective. For John, there is something perplexing about the light.

As well as this, John has other connections to make – with truth, for instance. In the light of what we have just said, John wants us to understand that the light is true – real, genuine – for truth is another of John's concepts that takes on a life of its own. It has, for instance, the capacity to set us free (John 8:32), and as a line of thought it crosses many of the other important threads that weave through the gospel. John develops this identification of light with truth as something good, by accentuating the connection between the darkness and evil. While we do not want to pre-empt the colour and atmosphere of Nicodemus' visit and the subsequent discussion, we can, at least, remember what Jesus says at the time (John 3:20): 'Everyone who does evil hates the light, and will not come into the light for fear that his deeds will be exposed'.

Finally, John makes the connection between light and life (John 1:4). It is a natural metaphor and, once more, to underline the connection, there is a story later on about a dead man that will demonstrate the linkage between light and life – firstly as the stone of his tomb is rolled back to admit daylight, and then as Lazarus himself emerges from the darkness of death. John is staunchly universal in making this linkage – the light is for everyone (John 1:9). Is this simply the capacity to sense things or feel objectively about them, the light that makes us human? And if so, does it light us up from the inside or from the outside? Is it like the light of conscience, which illuminates our choices, but which may be dimmed or extinguished with time and effort (1 Timothy 4:2)? And if the light has this universal dimension, how do we square that with the choice that we may make to avoid the light? It is not clear right now, so we must hold both to the universal element and the element of choice until it becomes clearer.

So then, we are hardly into this gospel before John has presented us with a bright image of light blazing away in the darkness. Naturally enough, he has connected this to the concepts of life and of truth. More surprisingly, perhaps, is the appearance of a witness to point to the light, because although the light is shed universally, it is not inescapable, at least not for now. The truth and even the life are both avoidable choices – we may step into the light but we don't have to.

## Night and Day

I hope this is not reading too much into the gospel to detect a photographer's idiosyncratic eye in the images. Clearly, there are some aspects of light and shade that all four gospel writers record – for instance, the night time arrest in Gethsemane (Matthew 26:47-56; Mark 14:43-50; Luke 22:47-54; John 18:1-12) and the series of trials that follows. However, John ignores the darkness that descends during the crucifixion (Matthew 27:45; Mark 15:33; Luke 23:44,45) as reported by the synoptic writers, even though it is a rich image. In what he avoids and in what he includes, then, John shows himself to be master of his material.

Sometimes John's allusions to days are not really part of the day/night imagery at all. He counts off days, for instance, in John 1 to provide himself with a marker from which he can arrive on the 'third day' (John 2:1) in Cana. While there is a degree of secrecy surrounding the social gaffe at the wedding, and the first sign that John reports, John does not seem to make much of the lighting.

He does make something of the timing of the light in the next story – Nicodemus' visit. That it was night is asserted at the time (John 3:2) and is underlined when Nicodemus' reappears later in the narrative (John 19:39 – although the time of day is not mentioned in John 7:50). So why does John want us to understand that it was night when Nicodemus arrived? Is it a visual commentary on Nicodemus' moral bankruptcy, or lack of knowledge? Is it because he is cautious, perhaps overly so? Is he frightened? Does John want an early example of someone who comes in from the night to contrast with Judas, who later on goes out into the night (John 13:30)?

What we do know is that the conversation turns in time to the topic of light and darkness – and it is dark outside. As a backdrop, it frames a commentary that is both forceful and moral in tone (John 3:19-21). There is a verdict – a point of crisis! Although the light has come, people love the dark. By contrast, those whose lives are governed by truth are prepared to step into the light. I wonder if there is a wry encouragement to Nicodemus to be a little braver. If so, it certainly worked (read John 7:45-52 and 19:38-42)!

However that may be, the passage clarifies one aspect of John's take on life and darkness – good and evil. This intensely moral view is also an 'out there' perspective. Just as the night is out there, the light is out there. It shines upon the individual, not out of him or her. It delineates and exposes without fear or favour. Yet the reaction, from inside, is often extreme – we love it or we hate it, we fear it or we embrace it. But we cannot turn it off.

## The Moral Light

This creates at least two problems for us today. First, we may feel uneasy with so strongly a moral case. Second, it is becoming increasingly dangerous for an individual to assert any kind of moral imperative – especially in relation to personal behaviour. We can come back to the latter problem when we consider how John approaches individuals and their behaviour.

While John clearly believes in a moral call on every life, he is reticent to condemn (John 3:17-18). So how do we read this? Well, it helps to sense the cold light of reality about John's analysis. It is not so much what is going to happen, or a moral judgement about to be cast. The light is on and things are as they are – the offer that Jesus makes is an escape from a situation that already exists (John 5:24).

John reserves his moral fire for those who have enjoyed the benefits of the moral light and yet willingly turn their backs on it. Judas is an obvious target – the one who is a devil (John 6:70-71), the thief (John 12:6), although John is surprisingly restrained about the betrayal (John 13:2, 26-30). The other examples are the factions within the religious rulers, with whom much of the argument takes place in John 8 and 12 – more of this later (chapter 12, *John on the Rulers*).

For John, the moral light illuminates his landscape – and it is unbearably bright. If Nicodemus, a Pharisee, cannot bear the brightness, who can? However, as we have noted, John is slow to moralise – particularly with individuals. He records encounter after encounter in which Jesus declines to point out to people the extent to which they are responsible for their own predicament, choosing instead to draw them to saving faith and effective worship. It would seem that the metaphor for John is more spotlight than light-sabre.

Nonetheless, morality is a dangerous business if the majority disagree with you – and John's Messiah stands opposed, in many minds, to Moses and Abraham. They do not like the new thinking and long to silence this unofficial Rabbi, with his offer of a new way to God. The lengthy and at times elliptic battle between them and Jesus is a protracted life and death struggle. For now, we note the danger of the divide between light and darkness.

In any society, there will always be a set of truths that is dangerous to discuss. There are places today where it is dangerous to assert the deity of Jesus openly, and in those countries God gives his servants wisdom as well as courage. Even where Christian values seem to have been most openly supported, there have been truths too taut to talk about. After all, Tyndale was not executed by atheists, nor was the universal Christian family a well-articulated truth in the US half a century ago when black churches were being burned.

John does not comment on how well or badly societies show up in the light, often because he is interested in the individual, but he notes that the light will show up something every time. Society needs to be challenged. It is difficult for society and more so for those who do the challenging, but part of the church's job is to bring that light into the locale.

John's whole thesis is that humanity has become disconnected from God and that reconnection can take place only through Jesus (John 14:6). Since God is moral, there is a moral dimension to our journey and the morality is bound up in the character of God as revealed through Jesus. If we are to follow Jesus as the way to the Father (John 14:6), we must do so on his terms, not ours, so the Holy Spirit reaches into our lives and creates a sense of need in the form of conviction about the way we behave (John 16:8).

I have just been reading Richard Layard's *Happiness*. What struck me about the examples he provides is how many of the Christian values I grew up with correlate strongly with happiness, right down to the fact that the happiest societies tend to have a high proportion of people who believe in God. I was particularly impressed by the negative impact of divorce upon societal happiness, and the positive impact of stable social and family relationships. Despite the rhetoric of decades, two-parent families consistently turn out the happier children. Giving really makes us feel better. Even more surprisingly, increased affluence has not been converted into increased happiness in most western countries. The evidence is that people really are objectively happier in some circumstances and more miserable in others.

For me, the book was a bright break in the grey oppressive relativity that I saw around me in the 1970s Britain of my teens. To me John comes across as the most reflective of the gospel writers. For John more than anyone else, life is a highly nuanced affair. Yet there are also universals in John's view and some things really will make us happier.

John's Messiah says, 'I have come that they may have life, and have it to the full' (John 10:10).

So, for John, the moral light is as natural as sunrise. It is not always welcome, but it is there. A couple of weeks ago I attended a planning session for our teaching programme in what is now a beautiful conference centre called Cumberland Lodge, in Windsor Great Park. I have been there several times, and always seem to end up in the same corner bedroom. Lying in that half-comatose state between sleeping and getting up, I found myself dreaming dreams in which I kept blinking and shutting my eyes. I can't remember the dreams, just this sense that I dare not open my eyes. As I came to that June morning, I realised it was because the sun was streaming through the massive windows and had slipped across onto the half of the bed where my head was lying. It was bright – too bright. Moving over brought temporary relief but soon I had to get up anyway. As a long-term strategy, the idea of simply rolling over one more time would not have worked because the sunbeam was slowly sweeping across the bed. For John the sun has risen, most notably on that Easter morning where, for one group of people, the darkness was dispelled forever – and he was one of that group.

## The Light of Knowledge

There is another theme alongside the moral light. If we return to Nicodemus – and he is a central character in John's narrative – the discussion begins with some gentle jousting about who knows what. Nicodemus 'knows' that Jesus is a teacher from God (John 3:2). Later on, Jesus returns his serve with a neat drop shot on the same theme (John 3:11).

The idea that our salvation lies in knowing a person, is one of the grand themes towards which John is working (John 17:3). It links closely with his concepts of truth and, as we have seen, the important matter of belief. While the theme of light-as-knowledge is a bit of a teaser in the Nicodemus narrative, it is much more obviously a factor in the story of the blind man (John 9). The miraculous healing provides a dramatic demonstration of one man's journey from darkness into light, where, amusingly and sometimes farcically, John keeps a record of what people know and what they do not know – the neighbours, the parents, the Pharisees and the man himself. In between are those light bulb moments when the man realises that he knows more than he thought.

Speaking of light bulb moments, I remember sitting in an exam room working my way through a statistics paper. If you interview a thousand people and get an average view, there is a way to work out how far this might be from the result that you would obtain if you could interview everyone. I had done the calculation several times in wading through past papers, but I had never understood what I was doing. I can still remember a sort of 'ping' when I realised, as I ground out the last piece of the question, what it was I was up to. Suddenly, I knew why as well as how.

There is an element of that to John's take on knowledge, but it is not just about things falling into place. It is about a person, and how the pieces fall into place around him.

## Daytime Night Time

The preamble to the story of the blind man (John 9:1-4 – see also 5:17) reminds us that the daytime is for working. In his commentary, Jesus echoes the gritty wisdom of the Preacher – do what you can while you can because the night of death is coming (Ecclesiastes 9:10). The light is active, vibrant, vocal. Ultimately, the darkness has nothing to offer and so, while it is daytime, Jesus gets on with the job. It may seem a little uninspiring, but the light is there to support a task. It goes with purpose – Jesus works because that is what he was sent to do. So, is the opposite to working, not working? Maybe it is doing bad things – Judas' dramatic exit from the upper room – 'and it was night' (John 13:30) – sets the light level for the rest of the book. Judas has a choice – the darkness is out there if he wants it – and he does.

However, it is not just about the light levels, since the resurrection narrative starts in darkness (John 20:1) and ends in brightest day, for Jesus really is the light of the world (John 9:5).

## Summary

The theme of light and darkness is one that anyone of us can readily spot, but it is also one that takes us quickly into the heart of John's thinking. We have followed through three key associations that John establishes: a moral association with the light with its attendance option to remain in the dark; an association of the light with truth as it reveals the world as it really is; and a link between light and life.

Surprisingly, John's light needs a witness – so keep an eye on the illumination as you read. John has his eye on you as a witness!

## QUESTIONS

1 When the Pharisees argue with the man who was blind in John 9, how much of what they know is not true? How does the man who was blind find ways to refute their so-called knowledge?

2 George Berkeley in the eighteenth century asked whether if a tree fell but there was nobody around to hear it, would it make a sound (read up or go online)? How does John's idea of a witness align with this philosophical question?

3 How has your experience of the light been reflected in the evidence of your witness in the past year?

4 As a disciple, how can you be light and truth in your environment? Looking back over the past week, to what extent have you been successful? What might you try next week?

5 What topics are dangerous to discuss in your circle of friends or colleagues? How does John's gospel give you courage to raise them? What will you do next time the topic comes up – even if it is only being trashed or dismissed by a colleague?

6 Are you enjoying life to the full (John 10:10)? If so, how have you gone about it? If not, what might you do to get closer to it?

7 When was the last time a friend, neighbour or colleague approached you cautiously to ask about something sensitive? How did you handle the discussion? In the light of John's narrative, what might you try next time?

# 9 | JOHN ON… THE HOUR

> Now my soul is troubled, and what shall I say? 'Father, save me from this hour'? No, it was for this very reason I came to this hour. Father, glorify your name! (John 12:27-28)

One of the intriguing ideas in John, is that of the 'hour.' Although the other gospel writers use similar language at times, John develops it as a theme with an unusual take. Clearly, the translators have a bit of a problem with the idea, since some have Jesus talking about his 'time' while others refer to his 'hour' – and you may spend a little time nosing around an interlinear version to see which you would choose. Then there is the imminent hour and finally, Jesus declares that 'the hour has come' (John 17:1).

So, let's follow the theme through:

i   Jesus tells his mother that his hour 'has not yet come' (John 2:4).

ii  Nobody lays a hand on Jesus because his hour 'has not yet come' (John 7:30).

iii Nobody seizes Jesus in the temple courts, for the same reason (John 8:20).

iv  Jesus declares that the 'hour has come' and discusses his reaction to 'this hour' (John 12:23-28).

v   Jesus opens his prayer with the same declaration (John 17:1).

What is happening here? Is this a way to build the tension – always pointing us forward to something that is going to happen? I tend to look upon 'the hour' with a sense of foreboding, but from our study in chapter 7 (*John on Glory*) we realise that Jesus has a much more complicated view of what was happening, and of what was about to happen.

It piques our interest as the hour approaches, silently and beyond the awareness of the cast John is describing. We have watched enough thrillers to know the basic rule of suspense. If nobody knows about the bomb next to the hero, then it may jolt the audience when it explodes, and the fall-out may carry its own emotional charge, but that is it. For suspense, however, everyone must know about the bomb, and the camera needs to pan across the detonating device – everyone has to be counting down while they watch. How many James Bond movies would have been impoverished without a bright count-down timer heading remorselessly to zero and attached to something explosive?

By John 12, the clock is suddenly ticking much more loudly (John 12:23, 27) and after so many things have climaxed, the weather calms as we move into the eye of the storm. Will the crowd make up its mind or career from one extreme to the other, insensitive to argument and responsive only to mood? Will it win out against its leaders? Will Jesus make it as a popular hero in the end? In a few verses, it will all go quiet for a while as Jesus and his disciples find some quality time together. Quiet dialogue, the ticking of the clock, and all the time those references to glory that is shortly and shockingly to dominate the scene.

And is that it? A literary device? Before we rush on, let us acknowledge that even a device such as this is evidence of John's mastery of the medium. The way that the narrative flows and builds is worth enjoying, appreciating, pausing to admire and slowing down with. So even if that were all, it would be quite something.

## Is There Only One 'Hour'?

We use similar phrases today – your time will come, his day in the sun, fifteen minutes of fame. Such idioms may refer to a specific moment – childbirth, for instance – or to a longer period. So, what does John mean? As we try to tease it all apart, let's consider a parallel case that John sketches for us around the theme, not of 'the hour', but of 'the time'.

Jesus' family want him to go up to the feast as part of the crowd (John 7:6-8). It is not clear to me quite what their motivation is, because John tells us about their scepticism – maybe they want a laugh, maybe they want a sign, maybe they want to be at the centre of whatever interesting events are likely to unfold. Whatever their motivation, Jesus declines, and uses an odd explanation – his 'time is not yet here; for you, any time will do'. Then, after the crowd has moved off, Jesus makes his own way to the feast, but with the delay, he does not start to teach until the festival is half over (John 7:14).

Clearly, although his family has heard him saying that no, he will not go, he has said, not yet. It turns out that 'not yet' is a handy pattern to look out for and that it helps us to understand the hour. So, when is Jesus in a state of 'not yet'?

i   Jesus had not yet reached the disciples as they rowed across the lake (John 6:17).

ii   The Spirit had not been given because Jesus had 'not yet' been glorified (John 7:37).

iii   Jesus had not yet entered the village of Mary and Martha (John 11:30).

In each case, something is clearly going to happen and does happen. However, 'not yet' refers to a range of conditions that trigger what comes next. I raise this pattern because, if we have a single event in mind when we think of the hour – Jesus' death, or resurrection, or ascension – it seems to me that we are locked into a rather rigid way of understanding the narrative. This is especially so when we consider the miracle at Cana, where Jesus argues that he does not want to intervene miraculously because his hour not yet arrived, and yet he performs many miracles before his crucifixion.

So, maybe 'the hour,' rather like 'the right time', does not always have to relate to one single trigger event. I leave the possibility open, because it might help to disentangle a range of references to his hour, starting with that first occurrence back in Cana at the wedding (John 2:1-11).

However, there is another connection that may also help, and that is the theme of glory. It binds this first 'not yet' narrative to the two times where Jesus declares that his hour is upon him, and it is the theme of glory. There is a discourse on glory (John 12:20-33), a dialogue even, with a voice from heaven, when Jesus first declares that his hour has come. Similarly, the prayer in John 17, which opens with the same declaration, is full of reflections on glory, past and future. Returning to story of the first sign, we read that Jesus 'revealed his glory' and that the disciples came to trust in him.

Perhaps 'the hour' is when glory is revealed – primarily in Jesus' death and resurrection and in creating a path for salvation, but potentially on other occasions, too. That way, the first reference at Cana would be a sort of preview or a foretaste of what 'the hour' would bring when it finally came. This approach to understanding 'the hour', vague as it is, has the benefit of providing a common focus without forcing us to think of one single event in Jesus' entire life, even though there is clearly a general pattern of anticipation and then acceptance and even embrace, leading up to Jesus' death and resurrection.

Support for this view comes from another 'not yet' that we have noted, but one that is not connected to 'the hour'. John is explaining what Jesus means by living water and states that Jesus is talking about the Spirit, but then he has to add that the Spirit has not yet been given because Jesus has 'not yet been glorified' (John 7:39).

So there seems to be a connection between John's idea of the hour and that of glory.

### The Unexpected Hour

If we follow this lead, then there is a sense of unexpectedness for Jesus about the first revelation of his glory – at least that is the most natural reading of the text. How this fits with your understanding of who Jesus was and is, is a more complicated matter. It will involve trying to work out who the Word was and is in becoming human. Does Jesus, for instance, know everything that will happen to him? It is all predetermined and independent of any human intervention? It needs thought.

So then, has the hour ambushed Jesus in some way? From the other passages, we may end up with a view that the hour is predestined. This first encounter with the hour frees us a bit from the inflexibility of that interpretation and offers us a more malleable view, perhaps, of what the hour might be or become.

Whether Jesus expects it or not, he is ready for what comes next and complies with the wishes of his mother at Cana. This is not a time where Jesus shows any open sense of destiny – no speech, no public prayer, no short message for those around. And yet, for a few of those around, there is a mysterious and lingering sense of glory to ponder.

## Before the Hour Comes

One of the things that most intrigues me as I read how John handles this idea of the hour is the way in which he uses it to explain why things happened the way they did. It is not just that Jesus has a sense of destiny, but also the way that John uses the concept as a mechanism that stops other things happening. For instance, twice John reports a group in the crowd ready to take matters into its own hands and twice they fail (John 7:30; 8:20). Why? Because it is not yet the right time.

So, does John believe that Jesus is very literally invincible until the hour comes, or is this another literary device by which he lets us know that we have not yet reached the grand finale? I find it hard to escape the conviction that John sees Jesus as being protected ahead of the hour, and to that extent, he is invincible. That is not to say that there is no literary angle to this, since the hour is certainly one of the mechanisms John uses to underline and highlight the importance of the events he records in John 19 and 20.

As the narrative develops, Jesus says things that are more and more provocative. Those who are provoked get nearer and nearer to a dramatic intervention, but somehow they just cannot manage to do anything. Finally, the dam bursts and all that pent-up fury breaks against Jesus and we realise that his hour has arrived. So, there is something almost visceral about the restraining force that holds back the opposition up to that moment. John senses it and he uses it to explain why there is no violent response to the claims Jesus is making in John 7 and 8.

Meanwhile, Jesus' attitude to the hour seems ambiguous, similar in many ways to what we noted when we looked at the theme of glory. As Jesus contemplates the hour, we see that he is repelled and attracted, enthralled even, by the event (John 12:23-33). He also looks past it with great joy to the glory beyond (John 17:1-5). By contrast, my emotional reaction to these events tends to focus on the sadness and the horror.

I cannot imagine that knowing the details about my own death would cast anything but a dark shadow over the rest of my life, and yet it looks like Jesus draws strength from the fact that his hour has not yet come. Jesus is free to preach, to teach, to argue and to explain with total impunity up until the hour.

### Reaching the Hour

When I travel, the end of my visit involves careful attention to the process of packing as I move all the bits and pieces closer to the case, ensuring that when I finally get dressed, the last couple of items to go into the case are the coat-hanger my shirt was on and my toothbrush. For me the puzzle is complicated because some things can be reached only when I am wearing my artificial legs and some things can only be reached when I am not, so the choreography needs thought. If you were watching the process through a time-lapse camera, you would see things, items of clothing, my phone, and perhaps paperwork that I have read and digested but am not yet ready to throw away – all this flotsam and jetsam begin to congregate on the bed and then migrate closer to the case and then disappear into it, so that at the last minute, everything is in there. Usually for me the business of getting everything ready to cart down to reception is a cheerful sort of time, because I am looking forward to getting home – I enjoy travelling, but I love getting home even more.

With a very much more complex mood and from the middle of searing pain, there is something of this type of planning in the gospel, culminating as Jesus hands over responsibility for his mother from the cross at the very last minute (John 19:25-27). John underlines this with the statement in the next verse: 'Later, knowing that everything had now been finished...' (John 19:28).

This type of countdown is a feature of many situations – leaving on holiday, moving house, or the last day at work. It would be nice to be able to do all the important things early on and leave a few trivialities for the end, but often it isn't like that. You can't do the closing meter readings until you are finally out of the house. You can't lock the house up until the car is finally packed and everyone is in it and you are within seconds of driving off on holiday.

This helps us to see why John 13-16 are so packed with detail and new revelations, and why finding someone for his mother to live with is left so late in the process. Yet Jesus knows that the hour is coming and it is clear that he has been planning for it.

## The Eye of the Hour

It's an obvious point but worth stressing that Jesus' passion and resurrection are the capstone of the gospel. Whatever else the hour may refer to, it certainly covers the events of that astonishing weekend. Everything before leads up to those days and everything afterwards flows from them or seeks to make sense of them. The glory is finally and shockingly revealed.

For the past few weeks, our screens have been full of major storms wreaking destruction across the Caribbean and Southern US – storms Harvey, Irma, Jose. The pictures from aircraft flying above Irma, and particularly those taken from space, show the thick ring of clouds and, clearly visible, the eye of the storm – a small, clear patch of weather.

It's a bit like that with John, who provides an unobstructed view just over 20 verses long (John 19:16b-37) of the Lamb of God dying to take away the sin of the world (John 1:29). He has taken us through the buffeting leading up to the hour and will go on to describe some of the whirlwind events that follow it.

For now, however, there is an unexpectedly brief and quiet view of glory.

## My Time

One last question: is there an hour for me and what should I do about it?

It looks like Peter is given a glimpse of his hour (John 21:18-19). I doubt if any of us would readily associate the prophecy that others would dress and lead him where he did not want to go with anything other than the helplessness of extreme old age. But John – perhaps writing after Peter's death – sees the tinge of a deeper glory, and the hope that goes with it. Taking a traditional view, it is Peter who tells us always to be ready to explain our hope (1 Peter 3:15).

So, how could we be more aware of our hour and be more ready for it? How will we know when an opportunity to glorify God will come up? Too often, I only realise afterwards – something was said or something happened and while I pondered how to respond everything moved on. However, occasionally I am encouraged when I get it more right than wrong. Recently I agreed to meet for lunch with a Christian I had only recently met. I had brought a couple of my books along to pass on and they were lying, face down, on the table. When the waitress arrived, she flipped the books over, read the titles, and explained that she wasn't very keen on Romans. So, was that the hour? The restaurant was empty but it was a little awkward because neither I nor my fellow-diner knew the other well enough to have a clear idea of whether we would go off in the same direction of witness.

For about ten minutes before we placed our orders, we talked with the waitress about faith – indeed, about faiths, for she had a culturally diverse background and had read widely over the years – and then we talked briefly about unusual ways to read Romans and then about a smallish church nearby that she cycled past on her way to work each day. A streak of glory? I don't know. I only know that I was not expecting it, but it felt right to pause and respond to the opportunity.

Could I experience more of Jesus' example of the sense of invincibility before the hour arrives? There have been many times when I might have been braver, or even reckless, had I really believed I was untouchable at the time. We will all have friends who have believed that God has told them to do something and they have stepped out and done something very unconventional which has not worked out. So, there is a fine line between a God-given assurance of invincibility and presumption or even fatalism. It's a hard call to make, but it is worth making it a matter of prayer. Of course, that kind of prayer may help us discover what it is that God has in mind for us and create in us a sense of purpose.

Jesus has a clear a purpose in doing his Father's will and in reaching the hour – sometimes he undertakes the good things needed in the opportunities that he encountered, rescuing the wedding feast, healing the blind man, feeding the hungry or preaching to the crowds. In other ways, John shows how Jesus also has an overarching sense of destiny. A prayer to understand our hour, when answered, delivers us from the two extremes of acting out of either hope or fear. It is a hard prayer but it is there for the praying.

So then, the hour forces us all to think about our end. The way that Jesus ties up all the loose ends is an example to us all. I'm not on top of this, since I do not know how well I will manage the business of dying.

Over the centuries, Christians have met this challenge in different ways. Some lived a life so simple that there was not much to tidy up. Others had their date with death set through martyrdom and had, presumably, an opportunity to set their affairs in order. In our day, many of us have sight of what is coming by way of a medical diagnosis. I remember attending a conference not long after a well-known health economist had died. One of the stories circulating was how he had completed his tax form shortly before he died to save his wife the trouble.

In a world of living wills and lasting power of attorney, of bucket lists, hospices and holding out for a miracle, we have a wonderful example of someone who brought everything together perfectly, just in time and to his Father's glory.

## On Reflection

John has lavished skill as a narrator in communicating about the hour. Intuitively we sense what he means because we use similar idioms ourselves, but as we try to pin it down, we have found John at his enigmatic best. Unquestionably, the hour is closely linked with glory, stern and dreadful as well as well as bursting brightly with unquenchable life. Finally, once the hour has come, we glimpse an unexpectedly quiet glory in unfathomable events.

## QUESTIONS

1 How much of the idea of the hour do other gospel writers reveal? Where do their narratives align with John's and where does John add something different?

2 How many ways does John refer to the passage of time in his gospel? How does his approach free us from wasting time on the one hand, or wasting our lives on the other hand by being so preoccupied with saving time and being busy?

3 What does the hour teach us about Jesus' sense of purpose in life? Did he have a single aim or many aims and what was it, or what were they?

4 Is it possible for a Christian to step out and do something dangerous with a complete sense of invincibility? If so, when? If not, why not?

5 What does Jesus mean when he tells his family that, for them, any time will do (John 7:6)?

6 When was the last time the hour caught you unawares? Describe how you felt and reacted.

7 How would you like to die? How are you living to make sure that happens?

# 10 | JOHN ON… ONE TO ONE

The Samaritan woman said to him, 'You are a Jew and I am a Samaritan woman. How can you ask me for a drink?' (For Jews do not associate with Samaritans.) (John 4:9)

I wonder what the most difficult conversation was that you have ever had? Not necessarily in terms of the subject matter, but because it was very hard to communicate. Maybe it was at a party with a drumming beat that forced you to clip your sentences and watch the other person's lips. Maybe the signal was too poor to support the video conference, maybe the line kept cutting in and out or, in the good old days, maybe it was just a very buzzy line. But most of the time, even in difficult circumstances we would rather talk than not.

In a sense, John's conversations come to us down a noisy line – the language in which they were first uttered is not the same as that in which they were recorded, and the language in which we read them today follows yet another stage of translation. We have no body language, no tone of voice, no clues other than words on a page.

And yet, as people we come with senses and a brain hard-wired for conversation – we pick up language instinctively and even in terms of the raw energy needed to register a signal, our ears are about ten times more sensitive than our eyes. In more ways than we imagine, we spend our days waiting for, deciphering, and pondering, the word. Perhaps in more ways than even John imagined, he is writing to people who are expectant for the Word.

In John we also have a master of narrative. He comes from a culture where people are used to telling stories – incidents of relatives, friends, and enemies – to keeping personalities alive around the table and in the market place. The line may be noisy, but the signal is exceptional. I wonder at times – and as far as I know, it is pure speculation – whether John as the youngest and perhaps most impressionable disciple took on more of Jesus' mannerisms than the rest. Perhaps in John we have an echo of Jesus that captures more of his personality than the other gospel writers, because more of that personality got inside the writer. To me, and I'm not an expert in psychology nor in the original languages, John's Jesus is more mysterious and elusive, certainly than Mark describes. John's Jesus has more up-close personality than Matthew or Luke reveal, even though they both give us swathes of his public ministry. It's a long shot, but I wonder at times.

## Life and Death Moments

For me, the most electric encounter is near the end of John (20:11-18) and the conversation flips in just two foreign words – one a name and one a term that John transliterates. They are not our words but they send a tingle down our spine: *Mary, Rabboni*! Up to that point it has been a conversation that was going nowhere – Mary thinks she is speaking to the gardener but this is not her only misapprehension. In the early light of a new day, she does not yet know that a very different day has dawned and that death itself is being rolled back.

In the early days of our marriage, Dani and I spent many a Saturday evening learning how to solve cryptic crosswords, sitting on the floor surrounded by a thesaurus and dictionaries of various types. These days we usually get quite close to the end in a fraction of the time and without reference books. Sometimes, however, something interesting happens – our brains will get to the right answer before either of us knows why – an unlikely word pops into one of our heads and it is only after it refuses to go away and we sit and unravel it backwards, that we understand how it is the right answer to the clue.

Something similar seems to have happened here, triggered by the spoken word: 'Mary'. Her eyes have not helped her but her ears do, because her world is turned on its head in just two words. It is not the content, but the voice that cuts through her despair and although she does not know why or how, she suddenly knows who: my teacher!

Although it is perhaps the most personal conversation, it is one of the briefer discourses that John records. It starts in confusion and ends in commission as Mary receives a message for the other disciples. In other conversations we may not be able to identify such a clear point at which the interview makes a similar transition, but this exchange epitomises the pattern of almost all the discourses that John records for us. Most of the time Jesus reveals himself to his interlocutor in unexpected ways and most dialogues move from a sense of enquiry to a sense of certainty. In Mary's case, it is utterly shocking and wonderfully surprising – here is a dead man talking.

The other great life and death passage in John tells us about Lazarus (John 11) and again, the conversations are brief but highly charged. Once more, just two words – 'Jesus wept' (John 11:35) – capture the emotion thrust. The poignant moment draws a line under the discourse and moves the narrative on to action.

Notice how John allows us to watch each of the sisters, Martha first (John 11:20-28) and then Mary (John 11:32-34), as they meet and talk to Jesus. Both conversations start in the same way: *if only*. The second conversation seems to be so brief and one-sided as not to be a conversation at all – for both sisters, the transition from grief, regret and looking back, to the present joy of a brother restored to life, comes not through discourse, but through a miracle. Two sound bites and then an explosion!

Well, not quite. John gives us one more conversation, or at least the half of it that he heard (John 11:41-42) when Jesus prays out loud in front of everyone. The silent response to that prayer is the demonstration of resurrection that follows immediately.

So, what does John expect us to glean from these vignettes? With Martha, we see what will become a familiar pattern, as Jesus wrestles with the individual's reason. Even in the numbness of what has happened, Jesus will not be content with platitudes or empty comfort and he works on her belief of resurrection. We don't realise how serious Jesus is about this until he orders the stone to be rolled back (John 11:38-44) and Martha protests that there is a decomposing body inside! Jesus goes back to the conversation – if she will believe, she will see glory.

That was the point of the stories – they were never about feeling better, they were about the world, their whole world, moving to a better place. Also, there is the reminder woven in that these conversations do not go anywhere without the vertical conversation of prayer.

The immediacy of resurrection sets the conversations in John 11 and 20 in a category of their own. In other one-to-one situations, the pattern is similar but the contrast between the start and the finish is more constrained. What else, then, has John to say? Of course, the funny thing is that John isn't saying anything! John is listening and recording it so that we can listen as well. So, what is there to listen to?

## Big Ticket Talks

John provides us with two extended and contrasting conversations, for Nicodemus (John 3) and the Samaritan woman (John 4) are a surprising pair: the man and the woman; the educated and the uneducated; the committed orthodox believer and the uncommitted heterodox believer. John is not the only gospel writer to put such material side-by-side, for Luke (Luke 1:46-79) puts the song of a peasant girl next to the composition of an educated priest, adding an extreme difference in age into the mix.

In their own ways, and by arranging this material early on in their gospels, Luke and John are underlining the truth that the gospel is for everyone. Through these example, Luke shows that his message will stir any heart to song – optimistic youth through to world-weary old age. Using a variant of the same stratagem, John shows us that there is a logic and an appeal through the Word that anyone can grasp.

Both stories start in a tense atmosphere. What is this man doing pitching up after dark? What does he want with his opening gambit about what he and his colleagues know? Is he trying to establish his credentials, Rabbi to Rabbi? For me, the line is really noisy – I just don't know enough about the culture. I know academics reasonably well and my guess is that many of those with the expertise to comment on this passage would be just as awkward in trying to set up a conversation with an unqualified genius… and many would not even see how ironic such an encounter would be for them.

The film, *The Man Who Knew Infinity*, captures something of this type of cultural abyss as it explores the relationship between Hardy, an Oxford professor played by Jeremy Irons, and Ramanujan, Dev Patel's maths genius from India who makes the trip from the edge of poverty to Cambridge. Ramanujan's ability to generate results without being able to produce the proofs is deeply frustrating to Hardy and the central enchantment of the film is the struggle between these two to communicate – for me the rest is mere noise, though wonderfully portrayed. My favourite part is about the cab (go online to find out about taxicab numbers), but it won't help us here.

The social awkwardness of a man and a woman from alienated cultures, silent and alone beside a well beneath a burning sun, is much easier to grasp, even if our culture is more inclusive these days. Presumably the build-up has been tense as Jesus sits by the well and the woman approaches with her jar to fill with water. Is he going to move away? Is he staying to keep her away? The problem here is not to cut through an avalanche of words and ideas, but to break the silence.

In each case, Jesus manages to do just that. He parries Nicodemus' opening statement with a statement of his own that moves the conversation from statement to questions. You may read this differently, but I cannot see that Jesus wants to establish himself as Nicodemus' equal, although Nicodemus may well have seen that as a great compliment. Jesus wants to reveal who he is and why he has come, and the fact that Nicodemus will take the trouble to sneak around one evening to find out for himself means that he is worth spending time with.

By contrast, Jesus breaks the silence at the well by breaking social convention and by identifying himself with this woman – she is clearly thirsty – he is, too! Once again, he is master of the situation and has turned the stand-off into something altogether more helpful – a question. Why would he speak, across the many divides of the day, to her?

I will leave the details of the discussion for you to explore, hoping that you are sufficiently curious by now to spend a little more time with these characters.

And the contrasts continue: Nicodemus disappears into the night and we do not even know how or when he takes his leave. We know that something clicks with him eventually because of his later appearances and behaviour (John 7:50-53; 19:38-42), but we have no idea what it was that convinced him, nor whether it was a flash of inspiration or a growing conviction. In a sense, this conversation is stretched across most of John's gospel. There is clearly a turning point and the discussion has been decisive, but we do know quite know how, when or why.

There is no ambiguity when it comes to this delightfully forthright woman and her water jar. She reasons, she is convinced by what Jesus knows about her, and she has sufficient background and faith to connect the dots up. She dashes off and soon the well is no place for a weary Rabbi as the crowds come out to meet him. However, the friendly swarm that trots over to see what is happening has that covered, too, and accommodation is found for a couple of days to hang onto this amazing teacher and the shocked crew around him. We hear the moment of change, we watch the results, it all makes sense.

## Something for Everyone

Nearly 30 years ago I listened to a radio interview of Billy Graham by Prof Anthony Clare. I remembered it as a session from a series called, *In the Psychiatrist's Chair*, in which Anthony Clare met people from all walks of life for a discussion about what made them tick, although my internet search indicates that this was a one-off interview in connection with a visit Billy Graham was making to London. There are traces of the event online, but I could not locate a transcript or recording.

I cannot remember all that was said, but I certainly remember the feelings with which I started to listen and my sense of relief at the end of the interview. My concern had been that Billy Graham would be taken apart by his well-educated inquisitor and I guess that I badly underestimated both parties in this conversation. What I heard was a warm and engaging story of Billy Graham's own conversion and the way God had led him from there.

Billy Graham's ministry around the world in the second half of the twentieth century tapped into this central theme that John noticed and put on show for us – a rational discussion can lead to a life-changing encounter for anyone. John knows that it will not work for everyone because he has seen people walk away. The lame man wanders off (John 5), as does Pilate (John 18:38). For the lame man there is too little else going on in his life for him to rouse himself to think, and for Pilate there is far too much, even though he gets as far as a seminal question about truth.

This leads to a critical question for us in our era, the first half of the twenty-first century – do we really believe that a rational presentation of, and dialogue around, the gospel leads to changed lives?

There is the archetypal caricature of the British man abroad who simply talks louder and perhaps more slowly in English when he does not know the local lingo. It isn't always wrong to turn up the volume, but the church in Western Europe and, for all I know, the US, has been increasingly guilty of the opposite absurdity – subsiding into silence when it has something to say.

John encourages us to hope that there is a message that makes sense and will change lives, all sorts of lives, across the spectrum. It can be articulated in a way that makes sense every time, even if it is not assured of acceptance each time. Increasingly Christians are being bullied and ridiculed out of their right to speak about what is happening around them. The secular world is also growing lazy and lumps together all acts attributable to religious belief, from the valiant to the vile, into a single category which it simply dismisses. If your argument has a religious connection, so the assumption goes, you simply have no right to speak.

So John reminds us, patiently and as he has done for nearly two thousand years, that if we can be bothered to think about the message and to take it out sensitively and with purpose, people will be changed.

## Learning from the Master

Clearly John has not written a manual, particularly not a Western 'how-to' manual, of the sort that populates airport bookstores. You know the sort – four-and-a-half easy steps to a (thinner, brighter, more successful, more caring, richer) you! However, it would be crazy not to stop a while to think at this point. This gospel may not be a manual, but that does not mean it has no method to describe. So, what is the method behind the pattern that moves many people in John on from uncertainty or despair to confidence and hope? Our concept of having a game plan probably comes close to this – a game plan is not a detailed schedule but it usually has a starting point and some idea of how we want the discussion, or sale, or whatever, to go.

In my teens, when I played chess poorly (I hardly play at all now), I learned a few openings. I did not learn as many as those who played rather better than me and I did not learn as deeply as I could have. But by learning an opening in chess, you recognise that you cannot think everything through under the pressure of a ticking clock. You certainly cannot follow through all of the combinations of the game in your head (nobody can, no matter how much time has been allocated to the game). So, learning an opening allows you to take shortcuts and to pause for thought as this particular position or that tricky combination looms.

From the reading I have done on how chess grandmasters think, it looks like having a deep familiarity with the positions that result from different openings provides them with a way of memorising what they see. When they look at a board, they do not look at the placement of each piece, but at recognisable clusters of pieces, often recognising the opening a position came from. They then use this insight to launch their analysis, building their play around positions that arise in common practice.

A vicar who used to speak at the Christian Union when I was a student did something similar – he told us how he liked to work from John 1 when having a first discussion with anyone showing an interest in Jesus. I have observed this pattern with other Christian teachers and evangelists – they have a story or a passage that they like to work with and they have developed such a familiarity with it that they can adapt the conversation quickly. Developed properly and used thoughtfully, a game plan provides the flexibility to be effective in sharing your faith – it is a comfortable outfit, not a straightjacket.

## Closing Sentences

John's observed conversations, usually one-to-one conversations, are one of the most intriguing features of his gospel. As well as drawing us in to admire and reflect, they encourage us to believe that we have a message that makes sense – we can have confidence in a rational explanation of the gospel and we can expect to see change. However, to make the most of the opportunities that come along, we may have to do some thinking, first. So here are some questions.

# QUESTIONS

1 Give an example of hearing a voice you knew, but at a time that you were not expecting it at all. What was your emotional response? How did the encounter continue? How does that help you to understand John's narrative of the resurrection on that first Easter?

2 When Jesus first meets Martha after her brother has died, why does he focus on the theology of resurrection with her? Why does he not just tell her that it will be OK?

3 Can you give an example of a conversation you have had that followed John's pattern in which uncertainty turns into a clearer understanding and even trust? You might like to think of medical encounters, legal encounters, trips to school, and especially conversations within the family. How did the conversation go and how do conversations such as that help us to understand John's gospel?

4 The oddest, and most contested, one-to-one encounter in John starts in a crowd and ends with just two people (John 7:53-8:11). Read the story and then identify themes that you have encountered in John that are present in this story? What is different about it?

5 Where do you think Western Christians have most lost confidence in the gospel? How would John want us to turn the volume up a little?

6 Jesus' early aim seems to be to encourage questions from the other party. Why does Pilate's question (John 18:38) not work?

7 What is your game plan for sharing your faith? Is it based around you own conversion experience, the conversion of a friend or relative, or do you go back to a psalm or passage of scripture? If you do not have one, how could you develop one and how might you use it?

# 11 | JOHN ON... THE DISCIPLES

Lord, what about him? (John 21:21)

By now you should have John down as someone who watches, who sees the world differently, who thinks about it differently, and especially, who watches people. I was once told that great minds talk about concepts, medium minds talk about facts and small minds talk about people. I realised instantly what sort of mind I had, because people are always the most interesting part of the picture.

This classification system does not work, however, when it comes to John because his gospel is full of big ideas – the Word, the hour, glory and, although we have not looked at it, love. Yet it is not devoid of facts, time of day, days after this, as well as numbered jars that had this in them until they drew it out and then it turned out that it was wine. There are dead men who have been buried and come back from necrosis as well as from the dead. Gloriously and supremely, his account is teeming with people.

Having looked briefly at the one-to-one encounters that Jesus has with people, let's spend time looking at larger groups, the disciples, the rulers, the crowd, the world – starting in the chapter with the disciples. The groups we will look at are not concentric circles, with each larger group including everyone on the previous one. In fact, some of the groups are quite distinct from others, even if there are overlaps, for instance, when rulers become disciples, or a disciple slips into the night to join a different crowd.

## The Women

There is no *John on Women* chapter in this book, but John gives air time to women and what they have to say: Mary at the wedding, the Samaritan who comes to the well, the sisters Mary and Martha, and Mary Magdalene. We have studied these, and will turn later (chapter 13, *John on the Crowd*) to the collection of women near the cross (John 19:25).

Luke identifies categories of followers in terms of three within twelve, a group of women, and a group that swells to 120 (Acts 1:14-15). John is less structured but he has a remarkable take: with the possible exception of the woman described in John 7:53-8:11, all the women John describes fit a single category – they all follow Jesus. This is not true of the Twelve, of the rulers, of the crowd or of the world. It is also unlike the men in John with whom Jesus' relationships are characterised by a range of emotions – from frustration and disappointment to anger as well as commendation, concern and deepest commitment. The women have surprisingly straightforward relationships with Jesus – direct, honest, intuitive and trusting.

## The Twelve

So then, what are we expecting John's take on the disciples to be? As he paints them onto his canvas, will they all be the same colour? Will he use a broad brush? How well does he know them, anyway? If we are to take John 21:24 at face value (and I'm content to do so), then John knows them rather well because he was one of them. However, he is so keen to cover his tracks that there is not a single named reference to himself or to his brother, James. According to the synoptics, there were two pairs of brothers at the heart of the group of disciples – Simon and Andrew and James and John, presumably Simon and James being the elder of the pairs. From the other writers, James and John appear to have been the more colourful pair, so much so that Jesus gives them a nickname – the 'Sons of Thunder' (Mark 3:17) – while Luke tells of an occasion when they were all for calling up a lightning strike against an unwelcoming crowd (Luke

9:51-56). Their mother is fiercely ambitious for her boys and asks that they might sit either side of Jesus in his glory (Matthew 20:20-23). The response she receives is an unexpected reply about drinking the cup Jesus will drink and, in a strange way, it looks like this prediction and their mother's request coalesce in an unexpected way as James becomes the first of the disciples to die – martyred by Herod (Acts 12:1-2) – while John, in exile, survives longest of the group. In doing so, the brothers book-end the era of the first disciples.

The Fourth Gospel is silent on this background and it is worth considering how such an outrageous and perhaps pampered young man could have become the reflective genius who produced this narrative. Even within living memory, we can see that a spell at university or in National Service allowed many young men to make it through a reckless phase and emerge more thoughtfully for life ahead.

This habit of hiding important details when they get too close to the author also forces us to guess from time-to-time – who, for instance, was the other disciple who was with Andrew when John the Baptist pointed out Jesus as the Lamb of God (John 1:35-42)? If it was John himself, it makes sense that he should have woven in his own story about how he met Jesus at the start, and it would also connect the two younger brothers at the heart of the group of disciples in a way that makes sense with what else we know – but it is speculation. At other times, John appears to disguise himself as 'the disciple whom Jesus loved' (John 13:23; 21:7, 20).

More mysteriously, although John refers to the Twelve (John 6:67, 70; 20:24), he does not name, as far as I can see, more than nine and, even then, he does not always use the names we are familiar with. My total in order of first named appearance, are: Andrew and Simon Peter (John 1:40), Philip and Nathanael – presumably Bartholomew (Matthew 10:3; Mark 3:18; Luke 6:14; John 1:43, 45) – Judas Iscariot (John 6:71), Thomas (John 11:16), Judas – Thaddeus and the son of James? – (Matthew 10:3; Mark 3:18; Luke 6:16; John 14:22), and finally, the sons of Zebedee (John 21:2).

## Silent Narrative

Even in introducing himself and his brother, John uses only a surname. The key effect of muting his own role and that of his brother, is that John can reveal subtleties in the stories of the other disciples. You know how it is in detective dramas when there is a tantalising phone call and eventually the technicians are able to take out the voice yelling for help and turn up the volume behind it, so that you hear a high-revving motorbike start up and ease off. We have a similar effect here and instead of building the story around two sets of brothers, perhaps with the younger pair being the wilder, and telling how three of the four became particularly close to Jesus and saw and heard things that the others did not, John is freer to explore other inter-relationships. Andrew, for instance seems to get on well with Philip and they appear together in tricky situations (John 6:7-8; 12:20-22). Meanwhile there is something else here, for it also allows John greater freedom to reveal people as individuals, not as part of a famous pair.

My Dad was a character with strong views who enjoyed – if that is the right word – a high profile in my parents' mission – he was admired and appreciated by some and treated with a degree of wariness by others. As a result of this, my Mom was often known as Harry's wife. When Dad died, she thought she might become her own person, but by then one of my sisters with her family had entered into a spell of ministry with the mission that would stretch for nearly two decades – and so Mom discovered that she was 'Dee's mum'. Now that my sister and her husband have moved into other spheres of ministry, Mom is the only family member associated with the mission, and as a retiree she gets to be a person in her own right. As John turns down the volume, and ups the fade on a dynamic pair at the heart of the group of disciples, he is freer to reveal the people he is watching, each as a character in his or her own right.

Surely there is more that we would expect of John – we would presumably expect insightful stories, one-to-one encounters. We might expect to get some insight into views they shared – the times they were mystified together, for instance: but we would also expect some of them to emerge from the crowd and we would, surely, hope to pick up their endearing idiosyncrasies.

## Questions, Please

Several characters emerge under John's pen who have remained largely invisible from the other narratives – let's start with Andrew, Philip and Nathaniel, who appears consistently together. Although the synoptics give roughly the same list of disciples, Mark's list is slightly different from the other two in splitting Andrew and Simon Peter up, so that Andrew appears next to Philip and Bartholomew (presumably Nathanael) – the latter pair appearing together in the lists provided by Matthew and Luke. Coming from a very different direction, John manages the same thing in connecting the three of them up in the first chapter of his gospel. Carson notes that the Greek is not clear here and a very satisfactory reading of the text is that Andrew first finds Simon Peter and then he finds Philip, who then finds Nathaniel. If this is so, it provides a nice connection between three friends at the heart of the group of disciples – a team that is hinted at in Mark – and not the conventional triplet we think of in terms of Peter, James and John.

Nathaniel turns out to be a bit of a shirtsleeve philosopher, musing about what Nazareth might throw up (John 1:45-51), but he is not simply into throw-away remarks, for we discover from his interchange with Jesus that he is a thinker and finds time to meditate – in many traditions this time of prayerful reading and thought is called a *quiet time*. Christians throughout the centuries have made time each day to switch off from everything else and spend time with Jesus. It is a habit worth developing.

I don't know what preconceptions we have of the people Jesus chose to follow him, but we may be in danger of assuming that Jesus chose blank slates on which to chalk up the message that they were to take to the world. This is not really the picture John presents. Andrew was searching and got as far as John the Baptist before he was pointed to Jesus. Nathaniel was meditating – presumably about Jacob and the ladder that went into heaven, from his first conversation with Jesus

– and is commended by Jesus for his high moral character. Someone else was with Andrew the day that John the Baptist pointed people out. Because the author of the Fourth Gospel is so slow to identify himself, it is probably not a bad guess that it was John – although that is not the only possibility and we will return to this question. Whoever the person was, it sounds like there was a group of friends at the heart of the team of disciples, each of whom was searching for something more in life, a group of seekers who had developed sound spiritual habits.

Nathanael is not the only one with questions and it is Philip who asks Jesus to cut to the chase and show them all the Father (John 14:8), and Philip, too, who works out quickly that there is no way they can cover the cost of feeding the crowd (John 6:7). Why is John interested in these interventions? In neither case has Philip asked the 'right' question or provided the 'right' analysis – presumably John recognises that, without a Philip, this group will never learn. Clearly, all of the disciples are at sea while they face the problem of feeding the crowd on the hillside or alone with Jesus in the upper room. What on earth are they supposed to make of Jesus' idea that the crowd needs feeding? Time to look around, expecting someone else to have the answer, or better still, to look inconspicuous! The same sense of not wanting to join in pervades the upper room, where the discourse is complicated even today, two millennia later, with the benefits of commentaries and the time to read and re-read the passage.

These moments call, not for the correct question, but for someone with the curiosity to ask any question at all in order to get things moving. Philip is one of those people. In fact, Jesus picks Philip out and asks him how they are going to buy enough for everyone to be fed (John 6:5-7). Clearly Jesus is interested in Philip's thought processes and keen to develop them. Would we have noticed that in Philip?

### Networkers

As we consider this, we see something else going on within the group. Andrew locates the boy with the loaves and fish, while Philip is trying to scope out the scale of the problem with Jesus (John 6:5-

9), while both he and Philip are involved in opening up an audience with Jesus for a group of visitors who had come to Jerusalem to worship (John 12:20-21). We have seen that Andrew goes to get his brother Simon, when first he meets Jesus, and we know that Philip goes to find Nathanael (John 1:40-51). We note that the passage, while complicated, allows for the reading that Andrew went and got Philip. These passages build up a networking picture – people who connect with other people. If you want to follow this up, there is a question at the end about how well we identify the networkers in our churches and set out to help them be more fruitful.

## The Traitor

Surprisingly, John mentions Judas Iscariot more than any of the other writers – not by a large margin, since Matthew is watching Judas, too – and it leaves us wondering why. The first time we hear about Judas, Jesus is telling the group of disciples that although he has chosen them all, one of them, 'is a devil' (John 6:70-71). Talk about a tense introduction! The second time he appears in the narrative, John brands him as a thief (John 12:4-6).

So, what do we make of Judas? What about a life that goes over the cliff? Was there more that could have been done to identify the signs? If John could see the signs and we can see the signs 2,000 years later, why doesn't Jesus intervene and change things?

There are so many questions to which we would like to have answers that John does not address. What was it like to have Judas around? Had the other disciples guessed early on that something odd was up? Was Judas an edgy character? Was he a loner? Did Jesus appoint him as treasurer to the group or did he simply appropriate the role?

We know more from the other gospel writers about Judas and that last, fatal deal with its exchange of coins and the remorse that followed, but John leaves all of that out. He seems to focus from the start on the behaviour that made Judas susceptible to the wrong sort of prompting (John 13:2), so that eventually Satan steps in and takes over (John 13:26-30). The emphasis on this moment when Judas takes the bread and departs into the night is surprisingly precise and movingly atmospheric – we never see Judas by day again. In his final scene, Judas and his new comrades are illuminated by torchlight (John 18:2-7).

Masterful storytelling, and a warning, too! Whatever your theology, here is someone at the heart of Jesus' ministry who drifts into bad habits, starts to make bad decisions and is unable to help himself when he needed the courage to back out.

## Peter

As we approach Peter, we already know a great deal about him from the other gospel writers. Peter is probably the one disciple most of us feel we could describe with a thumbnail sketch: gregarious, generous, a spokesman for the rest, and he clocks on sooner than most who it is that Jesus really is.

In the other gospels, Peter is the anti-Judas character, the one who denies his master and yet is rescued from despair. Judas goes down and out – Peter goes down and comes back. This, surely is one of the great mysteries at the heart of the group of disciples – how can two journeys which seem destined for the same end, reach such different destinations?

In terms of the main features, John develops the picture we would expect of the impetuous, outspoken and insightful disciple – see the question at the end – although there are times when he is surprisingly reticent to speak out (John 13:22-24). It sounds, from the narrative, that Peter and John were thrown together more in the final hours before Jesus' crucifixion, but as we would expect, John's depiction of Peter is in any case more nuanced than the picture provided by the others, and he references him more than any of the other gospel writers. More of his attention, however, is given to reporting how Peter was restored to a position of leadership, after his fall from grace, which is part of the point of that last chapter in his story.

## Fishing Trip

If the prologue is a work of genius, he has not lost his touch with his final scene as the darkness and exhaustion of the overnight trawl gives way to new hope with the morning breakfast on the beach and a thoughtful, if painful, walk along the shoreline.

In a sense, this last scene draws together all the themes that John has been writing about. It is morning, once more, and Jesus reprises a much earlier miracle, the one where, according to Luke, Peter made the break and decided to follow Jesus (Luke 5:1-11). The scene is old but not stale. It tingles with excitement, as John recognises the stranger calling to them from the shore. Yet it is also deeply mysterious – why on earth do the disciples want, but not dare, to ask who their host is (John 21:12)? Bubbling to the surface is something that John has been telling us all along, that these first disciples both understood and yet failed fully to grasp who Jesus was. Having completed the apprenticeship, on this graduation morning, they still do not understand completely who Jesus is.

Then Jesus and Peter peel away for a searching conversation about what has happened and what will happen next. John uses the same word for a charcoal fire here (John 21:9) as he did when describing Peter's three denials (John 18:18). Three denials; three restoring questions; superb narration.

Peter is tempted to raise questions of his own, but those questions do not really matter. There will always be things we do not understand, there will always be new encounters with Jesus, there will always be a future that we could not have imagined, there is always forgiveness for the past and a commission for the next step forward. It does not matter what others are called to, either. John watches Jesus and Peter meandering along the tideline, but Jesus' plans for Peter and for John are different, and neither should be distracted by the other.

Had we had a chapter on love (another one I am leaving for you) we might have watched John catching the threads he worked with earlier

– Father and Son, God loving the world – and winding them together into the cord that really connects us to this mysterious Jesus.

Discipleship for John is not just about being part of a group, a puzzled group at times, but about establishing our relationship with the one at the centre of that group. This really is a great place to leave John's gospel if you are an aspiring disciple.

# QUESTIONS

1 Given the reports that the other writers provide about John as a disciple, what evidence is there that he has changed since he was a disciple with the group following Jesus? Is there evidence that some of his key characteristics may have been enhanced over the years?

2 By comparing three lists of disciples (Matthew 10:2-4, Mark 3:16-19, Luke 6:12-16) with the disciples that John names, produce your own list of the Twelve. How much can you learn from each of them?

3 Of the 15 references to Philip the disciple in the gospels, 12 are in John – the synoptics mention him just once each in their lists of disciples. Why does John focus so much more on Philip than do the others? As an example, how does John help us to identify people who might help us in our Christian faith today?

4 Try to think of a good networker in your church. How well does the church or home group leadership try to use this characteristic? What have the results been?

5 We tend to think of Peter as bring impetuous, outspoken and insightful. Provide a story from John in which he illustrates each of these characteristics. If you cannot find a match in any case, why might that be?

6 Why does Judas go down and out, while Peter is restored? What history and characteristics might have led to the different outcomes? Why does Jesus treat each one that way he does?

7 Why, even at the very end of the story, do the disciples both recognise and not recognise Jesus? Was this a physical phenomenon, or will it always be the case? Have you experienced this and, if so, how?

# 12 | JOHN ON… THE RULERS

Have any of the rulers or of the Pharisees believed in him?
No! But this mob that knows nothing of the law – there is a
curse on them. (John 7:48-49)

Although the rulers are a larger group than the disciples, they share
the characteristic that they are not a regiment of identical thinkers.
There are groups within groups when it comes to the rulers, just as
we observed with the disciples, and although the thrust of the rulers'
activity was against Jesus, there are those who break ranks. Just as a
disciple slips into the night to navigate for the opposition, so John
reports a Pharisee slipping out of the night to meet Jesus and find
out more.

## The Mix

Even before John introduces us to Jesus, he reports on a group of
priests and Levites who have been sent to find out what John the
Baptist is up to (John 1:19). Presumably, the Pharisees described at
the end of the conversation are part of the same delegation (John
1:24). So, who commissioned the delegation?

The latest NIV helps us out here because it talks about the 'Jewish
leaders' in Jerusalem, but other translations simply say, 'the Jews' – a
term John uses liberally and in different ways, to describe: the
leadership (as here), Jesus' enemies (e.g. John 8:48), the Jewish
community in its religious observance (e.g. John 2:6), members of
the Jewish race (as opposed to for instance, to the Samaritans –
follow the term throughout John 4), and sometimes it is a way of

referring simply to those in the crowd (e.g. John 6:52; 8:22). If you are using the NIV (2011), then the difficulty has been eased in the translation, sometimes by using the word, 'leaders', and sometimes, to avoid repetition, by using, 'they'.

The formal Jewish leadership would have been the Sanhedrin – John describes some of what went on in at least one of its meetings (John 11:45-53; but see also 7:45-52). The Pharisees and Sadducees were represented on this council, and presumably it is cross-party groups of this sort who are referred to in the recurring phrase, 'chief priests and Pharisees' (e.g. John 7:32, 45).

## By What Authority?

We know from other places that these different groups were sharply divided, for instance, over the question of the possibility of resurrection from the dead. The Sadducees, though not mentioned by name in John, were the strong party associated with the temple, while the Pharisees, who are mentioned, were the party of the synagogue and the people.

So, what sends them off together to start quizzing this new baptiser at the start of the narrative, as we have already observed (John 1:19-28)? What prompts a group to come and challenge Jesus over his authority to clear the temple of its traders (John 2:18)?

Years ago, when I started to run a small research division, I learned something about management and failure, which is that you need not have too many failures to spend most of your time putting things right again. Failure swallows up a disproportionate amount of energy. Working as we were in research and development, taking risks to produce prototypes, and being in a poor bargaining position a lot of the time so that things were done on a bit of a shoestring, it was not long before I found myself running a steady stream of time-consuming damage-limitation exercises. There was a laser signal regenerator that we thought was a demo but that the customer had ordered to dump in the sea as an underwater link to an oil rig. There was the circuit board for a camera that had to be impossibly light and foldable because the customer wanted to put it into a satellite that would smash into an asteroid, taking pictures all the way in. Neither of these projects worked well first time and both consumed time to sort out. One ended with an unhappy customer and no more work, the other ended in a second project that I wanted to turn down but that my boss made me accept – we did well on the second project, so my boss was right.

The disproportionate impact of things going wrong means that leadership teams, of whatever hue and however optimistically and well-meaningly they start out, soon develop a wary eye for things that might go wrong. They start trying to head failure off at the pass and anything new becomes a threat.

The Jewish leaders are in a particularly difficult bind because in many ways, they are not masters of their own destiny. They have authority in religious matters, but must defer to Rome and whomever Rome appoints to look after the region for anything political. We know from Luke's writing that Pilate could behave in disgusting and provocative ways (Luke 13:1) and that it was not uncommon for rebels to gather bands of followers to fight for their rights – Gamaliel describes a couple of the colourful characters who came along from time-to-time (Acts 5:34-39). Keeping a lid on this uneasy equilibrium was a tricky task, particularly during the big feasts when the swollen population of Jerusalem was well fuelled with food and drink and full of fervour.

This dual sense of responsibility that lies upon the Jewish leaders – to guard the worship of the one true God under the occupation of pagan overlords and to keep the nation itself together – is clearly present as they view what John the Baptist and then Jesus are doing. Someone in John's circle, perhaps John himself (see John 18:15), has access to the inner working of the Jewish establishment and reports on these twin fears – that if Jesus carries on with his ministry, the Romans will destroy the temple and scatter the people (John 11:47-48).

## John the Baptist

The antennae of the establishment, all aquiver for signs of religious dissent or political action, soon pick out John the Baptist, whose ministry the crowds are trooping out to see and experience (John 1:19-28).

It is clear that the gospel writers think that John the Baptist is a more important person than we do. Using almost any search tool, it is not difficult to assemble a sketch of John the Baptist's life and ministry, nor to see why he would have appeared as a threat. He draws crowds in a politically and religiously charged environment. He preaches simply and directly, offering ideas that people can put into practice (Luke 3:1-18). He provides a practical way for people to show their commitment by being drenched in a river, seen as a stepping stone out of their old life and into something new, and he connects with the ignorant masses whom the rulers despise (John 7:47-49).

John the Baptist has a moral authority that frightens Herod and a public appeal that threatens the religious leaders. He goes to jail for speaking up on a moral issue that the establishment felt it better quietly to ignore (Luke 3:19-20), and he is beheaded because he continues to hammer at the same nail (Matthew 14:3-12; Mark 6:17-29).

John testifies about who Jesus is. The rulers are surprised because they saw neither John the Baptist nor Jesus coming. If you are running something that is well over a thousand years in the making, with a temple that has taken decades to develop and is still not complete, you like to be assured that the next generation of leaders have come from the right sort of background and are made of the right sort of stuff. However well they may have followed the priestly developments around John the Baptist's birth (read Luke 1), they seem to have lost sight of him once he disappeared into the desert (Luke 1:80), with his unusual outfits and diet (Matthew 3:4; Mark 1:6). They missed the forerunner and were naturally on the back foot when it came to embracing his message. Since a key element of his ministry was to point Jesus out as the *Lamb of God* (John 1:29), they are naturally suspicious of Jesus, too.

However, Jesus picks up this evidence when discussing John the Baptist with the crowd (John 5:33-36). It is a slightly elliptical reference, since Jesus emphasises John the Baptist's witness to the truth, but the connection is made, nonetheless. In fact, in this discussion, Jesus draws on two themes that we have already explored – the theme of a witness and the theme of light shining in the darkness. One line of tension, then, between Jesus and the rulers is that they did not see him coming. They did not see the witness coming and they do not even know where Jesus was born (John 7:52). Jesus is simply not who they think they are looking for.

Meanwhile, there is a second line of tension here, as we have noted, in Jesus' use of the imagery of the lamp – moral authority. The one who came to witness that the light has come (John 1:7) also carries a moral authority, and for a while the crowds responded well to him. As we have noted – and it is clearer in the other gospels – John the Baptist does what the rulers should have been doing. He calls people to repentance, helps them to get their lives sorted out before God, and faces down a political ruler over his private life.

Jesus takes the discussion further – it is not simply that John the Baptist has the character and courage to do what the rulers should have been doing, but that the rulers are not keeping the law they claim to be defending. Some of the most shocking things Jesus says about his opponents concerns the moral quality of their lives: they do not keep the law (John 7:19); they want to kill Jesus (John 7:19, 25; 8:37, 40); and they follow the devil's desires in lies and murder (John 8:42-47). Later, we discover they even want to kill Lazarus (John 12:10). Somehow, John argues, their moral compass has flipped! But most seriously, in Jesus' eyes, they do not accept him as the one whom God has sent and cannot therefore enjoy eternal life (John 12:44-50).

## The Man is the Message

Of course, it does not look quite like that from their side of the fence – as the guardians of the writings, they have an unlimited responsibility to keep the nation intact, even if it means depriving a few people of their lives – and they have one person specifically in view (John 11:49-53). Somehow murder doesn't seem quite so bad when it is your duty. Thus, the struggle becomes a difficult and detailed argument over whether Jesus has been sent by God and they have failed to see him coming, or whether he is an imposter. The interesting point about this argument is that it is not about who is right and who is wrong – most of it is a struggle to find any common ground for an argument at all.

The rulers would undoubtedly have found it easier to debate propositions with Jesus – his take on Moses, the prophets, the psalms. They could have worked out whether he was 'sound' or not, and if not, they could have codified exactly what his problem was. However, Jesus does not give them that opportunity. Instead, he makes claims so wild and personal that they do not really know where to begin.

As we would expect with John, clarity comes in the last third of the gospel and Jesus is unambiguous with his disciples in that last discourse in the upper room, where he claims to be the way, the truth, the life (John 14:6) – not that he points the way to truth and life, but that he is all three. Working back, we catch the clash of expectations and the frustration that it brings – their bewilderment about who Jesus is (John 8:23-29) and Jesus' claim to be the source of satisfaction (John 7:37-39). It is all there.

### Slow Burn

Although it does not look to us like the debate is going anywhere, there are people who are deciding that this man might really be God's message. The establishment thinks it has maintained a consensus against Jesus that no thinking person has broken (John 7:48) but they are wrong. Even some of the leaders are beginning to put their faith in Jesus (John 12:42). We know of two – Nicodemus and Joseph of Arimathea – whose minds are changed as they follow the discussion and weigh the evidence.

These men are at home with decision-making at a high level. Both know how dangerous it would be to show open support for Jesus against the establishment, and yet both are prepared to show their hands at an appropriate time. Nicodemus does so initially in the most powerful way that anyone can contribute to a debate – he asks a question (John 7:50-51). It seems an innocuous question and it appears to be brushed aside as inconsequential, but questions are funny things. Some questions are like armour-piercing weapons that are designed not to explode uselessly on the outside but have a delay built in so that they explode later. The time-delay fuse in this question is that they have never met Jesus up close and personal – Nicodemus did and he took away enough for him to make up his mind in the end. They have gathered information about Jesus, they will trade arguments in public, but they have not taken the trouble that Nicodemus took to meet Jesus as a person, not just as a proposition. Had they done so, they would have realised that it was the meeting, not the argument that mattered. It was a great question.

Because of this, when things later come to a head the establishment is unable to marshal its arguments in a way that makes sense to Pilate. In the end, the debate dissolves into the only argument that can prevail – the monotonous chant of a mob (John 19:12-16).

Let us return to Joseph, who was on the council (Mark 15:43; Luke 23:50-51), and Nicodemus. After Jesus' crucifixion, they set about what they think is a hasty pre-burial, but a temporary burial turns out to be all that was needed (John 19:38-42) – although it was not the preparations that were brief in the end, but the death. This action took courage and represented an open break with the rest of the rulers.

By the things they ask and the way they act, they step away from their colleagues, and they step into something that is growing.

## Other Rulers

John tells us of a 'royal official' whose son was healed by Jesus, even though he was some way away. I have no idea how this person fitted into the network of important people, but he is someone who manages to avoid the struggle and comes straight to faith (John 4:46-53). His is a straightforward story – he approaches Jesus as someone who can solve a very personal problem. He thinks Jesus will be able to do something for him and when he asks, Jesus acts. Not every ruler has a complicated relationship with Jesus!

Herod might well have been disappointed that John has ignored him altogether, while Caesar only makes a fleeting appearance in discussion at the end as a goad to Pilate, whom the establishment is seeking to force into action.

There is, however, one more ruler....

## Watching Pilate

The last ruler that John watches is the representative of Rome – Pilate – who manages to have a private interview with Jesus. John's dark humour is evident as he describes the Jewish leaders wanting to avoid the ceremonial uncleanness of entering the governor's palace, while at the same time trying to push an execution through quickly and quietly. You will have to look around to see what sort of uncleanness the leaders were trying to avoid, but it provides John with another example of how easy it is to keep to the programme and lose the plot. This divide, however, separates Pilate from the group of leaders when he interviews Jesus – Pilate is in the palace and has Jesus brought to him, while the leaders stand outside.

Unlike the royal official we have just looked at, and just like the establishment standing outside the palace, Pilate approaches Jesus as a proposition and with no obvious sense of personal need, but Jesus can never be a saviour to those who have no need to be saved. The proposition that Pilate must grapple with is whether Jesus has committed a capital crime against the Roman state. Having listened to Jesus, he is rapidly convinced that there is no case to answer. Jesus' claims that he has come from another world do not worry Pilate at all, even though this otherworldliness is deeply distressing to those standing outside.

Political decisions, however, are not made in isolation and in the end, perhaps to his own surprise, Pilate goes the other way in his judgement.

That Pilate is intensely annoyed with the establishment is evident right from the initial stand-off: 'What's the charge?' 'We wouldn't have brought you an innocent man…' (John 18:29-31). It continues with the epigram he publishes above Jesus' head as a statement of his crime – Jesus of Nazareth, the King of the Jews – and his unwillingness to do anything about it afterwards (John 19:19-22). Doubtlessly, John views the description as one of those strange prophecies where someone gets it right in the middle of getting everything else wrong – but it is not hard to see why even a thoughtful, well-disposed governor would not appreciate being hauled out of bed to go outside and negotiate with a crowd who want an execution and who want it quickly.

Nearly 40 per cent of the gospel references to Pilate are in John's gospel, so John is clearly watching Pilate. Pilate is an interesting character – John misses out brutal events that others relate and includes material that the others do not. Pilate almost gets there – he is persuaded at one level and dissuaded on other grounds.

## Stepping Forward, Looking Back

John's take on the rulers is not an analysis of leadership, but he makes some observations that apply today. If you are leading a group of any sort, you might like to reflect on how to avoid the defensive pitfalls of opposing new things simply because you can see dangers to them, and to work out when to stop debating issues and find time to meet a person for yourself. Too often, we bear an uncanny likeness to John's portrait of his contemporary leaders, and not in the best of ways, either.

However, that was not John's main purpose in writing, and we have seen that John's groups always have those who come forward and those who turn back. Among the disciples, there is Thomas who gets there in the end and Judas who goes out into the night. The blind man develops eyes of faith, while the lame man by the pool can never step into a life that is truly new. Among the Jewish leaders, Nicodemus and Joseph decide to follow Jesus, while Caiaphas and many of his colleagues do not. With more secular rulers, the royal official sees Jesus as a saviour and is saved, while Pilate sees him as a puzzle that he cannot solve.

For John, it is not about the argument, it is about meeting Jesus and being in the right frame of mind when you do so. John's decision-makers are not always swift to their conclusions, but they are very sure afterwards.

## QUESTIONS

1 To what extent is the experience of the Jewish leaders in starting with excessive vigilance and backing themselves into a corner of inescapable hostility a feature of any leadership? Can you think of examples from politics and even from your own church life where the same patterns emerge?

2 How can church leaders know whether something new is from God? From your own experience of leadership, or seeing through the eyes of a friend who has been a leader, can you think of an example where a leadership got it right and one where it got it wrong? How do you know which was which and what were the key features of each decision?

3 Why do Jesus' claims about himself seem particularly hard for the establishment to argue with? Consider, for instance, his claim to be from above while they are from below, or that the Father (whom they cannot see) supports all he does (e.g. John 8:23 and following).

4 Consider the leaders who put their faith in Jesus – what do you think persuaded them?

5 When Caiaphas reasons that it is better that one man die than that the nation be destroyed (John 11:49-53), John sees this as a prophecy. What did Caiaphas mean when he made the statement and what does John take from it?

6 Why do those who approach Jesus with a sense of need tend to come away with faith more often than those who want to describe Jesus as a set of facts?

7 'What is truth?' (John 18:38). Should Christians be concerned to present truth in an objective sense? If so, what truths are important to fight for today? If not, then what?

# 13 | JOHN ON... THE CROWD

Very truly I tell you, you are looking for me, not because you
saw the signs I performed but because you ate the loaves and
had your fill. (John 6:26)

It is impossible to read the gospels – especially the synoptics –
without sensing the pressing presence of the crowd as it streams out
to be baptised by John the Baptist and listens to his direct talks from
the river. Houses overflow to the extent that someone is lowered
through the roof. The crowd forces Zacchaeus to run ahead and
climb a tree for a view of Jesus, while a shy woman with an
embarrassing problem sneaks through the crowd for a healing touch
– for a moment it looks like the crowd will come to her rescue and
shield her from discovery. None of these claustrophobic events are
related by John.

Last Sunday I went to a church I had never been to before because
a friend of mine was speaking there. The congregation had
outgrown their modest building and were meeting in a school, so we
duly sat in the Assembly Hall, which was adorned with student
artwork. While I enjoyed what was a long service for me, I also found
time for my eyes to wander over a selection of the best paintings
from the year groups who would also have sat in that hall during the
week. I liked the clever artistic ideas even when the technique was
clearly still under development. On my side of the room there was a
structured head of a girl looking out and laughing at the viewer. It
wasn't cubism, but it was heading that way, and it provided a lovely
complement to the worship we were engaged in.

Further around, there was a picture that looked like it had been produced by Minecraft™ (look online yourself if your children are not building their own worlds with it already). I realised that the shifting grey silhouettes in the picture were people. In fact, it was a crowd, looking with the viewer toward a central building, and I realised that John's crowd is a bit like that – it takes you a minute or two to realise that there is a crowd at all. This is often because, as we have noted, John focuses on an individual or a group within the crowd, rather than on the crowd as a whole. In John 1:19-28, for instance, there is clearly a crowd, but the dialogue is between John and representatives of the establishment, a passage we looked at in chapter 12 (*John on the Rulers*).

That there is a crowd is evident from the fact that John was baptising – an inherently public and open activity. But we also know there was a crowd because Jesus goes back to that same place later on and the crowd remembers John's preaching (John 10:40-42). What the crowd remembers, however, is not what we would have expected from the other gospels. The crowd remembers that John pointed this man Jesus out, and made some spectacular statements about Jesus. And Jesus – again as we noticed in chapter 12 (*John on the Rulers*) – picks up on John's ministry in his discussion with then crowd, or at least with a group within the crowd (John 5:33-35).

John's style of shading the crowd in, almost invisibly at times, is evident again towards the end of his narrative, where Jesus refers to the crowd who have heard what he has said, openly, in the synagogues and the temple (John 18:20-21). John's depiction of the crowd may differ from that of the other writers, but the record of a life lived in public and for public consumption is well aligned to theirs. So then, the crowd is not quite so visible in John as it is in the other gospels, but it is there in shifting silhouette.

### Feed Me!

Much of Jesus' ministry is conducted in public, but the crowd – the 'great crowd' (John 6:2, 5) – has its day beside Lake Tiberius.

The trouble with crowds is that they are full of people with competing and diverse interests. As we have seen, the rulers in the crowd have particular tastes and want the discussion conducted in a particular way. When they are nearest to Jesus, the arguments run along different lines from when the ordinary people are trying to get close. The crowd contains so much diversity that it is not possible to meet everyone's requests at the same time. John handles this difficulty by bringing the different voices in the crowd to our ears, each in a degree of isolation.

So, what is the common denominator – what do most people want? It would be tempting to follow Maslow's hierarchy of needs (look online) and for those who like that sort of thing, there are a couple of questions at the end. It would be tempting to place the people at large with the most basic needs – they want to be fed. Certainly Jesus feeds them on occasion – moreover, Jesus is aware of just how strong our need is to be fed, to drink, to be sheltered – so much so that when the crowd scouts around afterwards to find him and finally locates him on the other side of the lake, he notes that they are more motivated by the food than by the spectacle (John 6:25-27).

Is that all they want? Clearly not, because Jesus, as he did with the Samaritan woman, turns the discussion from the physical to the spiritual. Just as the well water would alleviate one's thirst for just a short time (John 4:13-15), so Jesus can encourage the crowd to strive for food that lasts into eternity (John 6:27). He can do this with confidence, because he knows that there is a spiritual appetite lurking inside each of them. They could enjoy John the Baptist's message because they were looking for something else (John 5:35).

Sure, some went out to the lakeside out of curiosity, to see what the day would bring forth. Most people in a crowd would have had a question, perhaps not fully formed, in their minds as they trekked out to be baptised by John or to listen to Jesus. They were expecting a prophet and the question about whether they had found him was always rippling along the edges of the crowd.

Those who were part of John's own crowd, the inner circle of disciples, picked this up when John the Baptist pointed to Jesus. Andrew's news to his brother is that the Messiah has appeared and, using different terms, Philip has the same story to share with

Nathanael (John 1:41, 45). The Samaritans are looking for the Messiah, and so the question edges around that crowd as well (John 4:29). Later, when we come to the crowd's reaction to what Jesus says in the temple, the question of whether he can or cannot be the expected prophet is swirling everywhere (John 7:40-42). Later still, the blind man believes he has been healed by a prophet – that's what prophets do (John 9:17)!

The memory of a meal may have driven the crowd to find Jesus, but it was their hunger for answers that drove them out there to need feeding in the first place.

## Living Water

John's other big crowd scene is the dramatic intervention Jesus makes at the Festival of Tabernacles. John draws out the tension with skill by relating a semi-private falling out Jesus has with his family – everyone is expecting something spectacular at the feast, why not oblige them? Jesus waits until after they have set out and it is not until the festivities are half over that he makes a very low-key entrance (John 7:14-52).

Meanwhile, John relays the 'whispering' of the crowd – will he, won't he? Is he, isn't he? What is going to happen (John 7:12)? What happens is what always happens when Jesus is in front of a crowd – he teaches! The temperatures rises and many believe. Eventually, on the last day Jesus makes an explosive call to those who want satisfaction, and once more the crowd is divided – some are convinced, others not (John 7:31, 37-44).

An interesting section of this crowd is a detachment of temple guards, culled as I understand it from Levitical ranks and at the establishment's disposal. They have their orders to bring Jesus in, they stand and listen, they return empty-handed (John 7:45-52). No Roman soldier would have behaved in this way – for one thing, the punishment for delinquency was too high (see Acts 12:18-19 and what Herod did to the soldiers guarding Peter when he escaped). Whether this group of men is curious or hungry we do not know.

Whether these guards wanted to hear Jesus or not, we do not know. They did not choose to be part of the crowd – they were there because they were there under orders.

Maybe they realise that they are the only ones in the crowd who cannot simply watch what is happening. Maybe they don't. But the fact is that they cannot sit on the fence because, for them the fence has been taken away by their orders. We may think them the most unfortunate of listeners because they do not have time for reflection. They cannot listen and walk away. Like the blind man, they are at a point of crisis, a crisis created in part by others – they are caught between Jesus and those in authority and like the blind man, they realise that they see things differently now!

Their orders create a crisis in their minds that others are going through at different times in John's gospel. They must act – and whether they do so actively or passively, they will have made their decision – and they have! They return empty-handed.

In this group of guards, we see the role that crisis can play in helping people to step out in faith and follow Jesus. Not everyone seems to have as serious a crisis and we have noted that some people seem to move quietly from one fixed position to another. Nicodemus, as we have seen, is a bit of an enigma, although it is a pair of crises that help us at least to see how his thinking has moved on. Perhaps, here, as he sees the plight of these guards before their commanders, we are actually witnessing a critical crisis in Nicodemus' own experience. By the time of his next public crisis – deciding to step up with Joseph of Arimathea and ask for the body of Jesus – his decision has clearly already been made (John 19:38-42).

Maybe there is also an unexpected domino effect in this story. Maybe Jesus sways members of the crowd as he teaches, and the temple guards are swayed in their turn. Their reaction when they return seems to have an impact on Nicodemus and he finds himself speaking up. This bottom-up connection, starting with the crowd and ending with a ruler, is a pattern that has occurred in revivals – George Whitefield and DL Moody being key players in such movements – where many ordinary people are converted, while a smaller number of the establishment come to faith.

## In Crisis

One last, tentative idea around crisis, and then we must move on. We see people around us who lurch from crisis to crisis and, for instance, each year I have a trickle of students who visit to talk about the problems they face. Usually they start pitching up when coursework is due or when an exam looms, and some of their situations are exceptionally difficult. Sometimes the string of crises seems to me to be partly of their own making, although I can see why it does not look that way to them. At their most extreme and in some of the saddest cases, they relate how their response to one crisis has catapulted them into another, until eventually they find themselves in a terrible predicament.

I don't think John is promoting a view that you must reach a crisis to decide to follow Jesus, although for many of those whom he observes there has been a moment of surprise or even shock that leads them to step out. Not every crisis leads to deeper faith – at least not directly, as Peter's unfortunate experience in the courtyard shows (John 18:15-18; 25-27) – but John is certainly alert to the potential upside of a good crisis.

Many of us will have encountered the idea of a crisis as a route to salvation. In some Christian cultures you had to be able to point to a moment of crisis as a necessary part of your conversion narrative or testimony. That some people experience a crisis in coming to faith is simply one of the things John observes and passes on.

I think there may be a slightly wider point here about making decisions, which is that if we allow God to work through the crises in our lives, we may do surprising things. The guards' crisis appears, perhaps, to have triggered a crisis for Nicodemus, who in turn joins with Joseph at another time of crisis.

Maybe it is the crisis at the end of the feast that helps Nicodemus to realise that he really can't go along with his fellow-rulers in their obstinacy and narrow-mindedness. Maybe as he approaches Pilate he suddenly realises he has become a braver person than he was.

As a late teenager and very early into my twenties, I enjoyed several holidays for thalidomide children run by an amazing woman, Ma Venning, who co-opted family, friends and assorted others to the cause of helping her out. She was a devout and very English woman who lived and operated within the establishment, and yet she told me that in running these holidays she had discovered new things about herself. Although a law-abiding road-crosser, when faced with getting a line of wheelchairs and people on crutches across a main road in London, she found herself holding up her hand and marching forth – and the traffic would stop! No time to evaluate a range of strategies for making it across, and so she just stepped out and everything was fine. I am not sure whether the small crisis of getting to the other side made her braver (even less law-abiding) or helped her to realise that she had become so. But clearly there is a link between crisis and development.

My experience is that I usually want to avoid the crisis or that I feel it has come too soon. I want more time to decide and to be able to set up a series of balanced options so that if one fails, I can move onto the next. As I write, there is some insecurity over my job. I don't have a problem with recognising that it may be time to do something new. What I would really like is another year or so to set things up. I may get that – I do not know. Reflecting on the decisions that people make in John, I can see that the crisis can, in God's hands, lead to great results. Some people have been filtered out of the crowd and are trickling into salvation, just because of a crisis.

## Women in the Crowd

John's scene of crucifixion is another one where the crowd has been muted as John turns down the volume and matted out with the broadest of brush strokes. The taunts and abuse recorded by others are absent in John. But he chooses two groups of people to paint in with care. He records the soldiers going about their grim business, although he does not report on any of them changing their minds or reaching a verdict about Jesus (Matthew 27:54; Luke 23:47). John's main purpose in watching the soldiers and writing what he saw seems to be related to his agenda on evidence – the flow of blood and water, establishing that Jesus really died (John 19:34).

The other component of that crowd was a group of women, of whom John refers to four, although working out exactly who they are is not without its problems (John 19:25). John's reasons for mentioning them is presumably that they provide evidence of the other half of the resurrection puzzle, for it is a group of those women – and John focuses on one of them, Mary Magdalene, in his resurrection narrative – who are first to the tomb that first Easter morning (John 20:1-18). The soldiers in the crowd provide the evidence that Jesus has died and the women will furnish the first evidence of resurrection (see chapter 15 *John on Evidence*).

## The Wisdom and Folly of the Crowd

The appetite of the crowd is always extreme because the tastes of the various factions differ in the extreme.

One need not read much of, or watch many plays by, Shakespeare to recognise earthy humour sitting next to profound insights and soaring verse. James Gillray, the satirical cartoonist who was at the height of his powers in the two decades spanning the eighteen and nineteenth centuries, has a similar way in his graphic art of addressing sophisticated political situations using rather crude caricatures of famous people. Each in his own way recognised the fragmented make-up of the crowd, and offers something for each constituency.

As he watches the crowd, John is clearly aware of the factions and he sees that they are often at war with one another – the temple guards are wary of the establishment, while the rulers despise the mob. He does not try to identify with any of these groups nor to exploit the differences between them. He is not out to entertain the crowd nor to back a winner from within its ranks. Nor does he caricature the different groups. The common people want food and signs, but they are also searching for moral guidance and particularly for the Messiah. Nor are all the rulers interested solely in debating the finer points of theology – one royal official has a dying son and comes to Jesus in desperation.

John is alert to the fact that there are always those in the crowd who slip over from curiosity to belief. Some see the signs early and believe (John 2:23); some have come to the temple to worship at the feast and they believe (John 7:30-31); some put their trust in Jesus as he preaches and argues (John 8:30); some see the miracle at Lazarus' tomb and come to faith (John 11:45). Lazarus himself becomes an object of the crowd's curiosity and many 'go over' – a strange but fitting description of the process – to Jesus and put their faith in him (John 12:11).

Some of these people reach an obvious point of crisis and step out. Some convey their questions or commitment in whispers that animate the crowd. For John, the thing about the crowd, as with any other group, is that some people come to faith in Jesus.

# Questions

1 Do you like John's depiction of the crowd more or less than, say, the way in which Matthew describes the crowds? If so, why? If not, why not? How does John show himself to be a master story-teller in the way he tells us about the crowd?

2 Look up Maslow's Hierarchy of Needs, which describes a set of needs that start with the basics – food, shelter – and works up to 'self-actualisation'. How does a hierarchy of this type help to classify the needs of those John encounters in the crowd and in other groups?

3 What is the relationship between 'low level' needs (for food and water) and 'high level' needs (for spiritual fulfilment) when Jesus is at work in the crowd? How should this drive our own efforts in evangelism and supporting the needy?

4 What can we learn by the fact that most of John's crowd scenes pick out a few individuals within the crowd?

5 What crises have precipitated decisions in your life? Which decisions have worked out well and which have turned out badly? What are your conclusions about making decisions in the middle of a crisis?

6 What do you think is the role of crisis in conversion? Try to consider cases where there was an obvious crisis and cases where perhaps more subtle factors were in play.

7 When it comes to matters of faith, to what extent do you think the crowd follows its leaders? To what extent do leaders follow the crowd? How might this help us to understand the role of the church in society?

# 14 | JOHN ON... THE WORLD

For God so loved the world that he gave his one and only Son, that whoever believes in him shall not perish but have eternal life. For God did not send his Son into the world to condemn the world, but to save the world through him. (John 3:16-17)

You might not spot the word John uses for 'world' on the printed page, but you would certainly recognise it if someone read the Greek text out to you because it is has come through to English as 'cosmos' and describes all there is – cosmology, for instance, studies how everything came into existence, not simply our planet or our world.

John is very interested in the world – his gospel uses the word, 'world' 78 times, although you will have to look at the Greek – perhaps online – to pick up all the references, because the English translators have eased out a few repetitions to smooth the narrative. His gospel uses up more than 40 per cent of the New Testament's allocation of the word, 'world' and if you include the other writings traditionally attributed to him, it is more than 50 per cent! Clearly, we are onto something fascinating.

As we noted earlier (chapter 12 *John on the Rulers*), John can use the same word in different ways. I don't know how many categories you would feel comfortable with, and you may have to consult a commentary to satisfy yourself, but here we will look at three. We will look at the world as a physical place – a world with room, a stage, if you like, or storage space. Then we will consider the world as a world of people, full of people, all kinds of people. Finally, we will think of the world as a system, a system of thinking and behaving that opposes Jesus.

## A World of Room

The first use we want to consider – ironically exemplified in the last occurrence and in the very last verse of the gospel – is simply the world as a physical place – our world (John 21:25). There isn't enough storage space in all the world for all the possible books about Jesus. Earlier in his gospel, there wasn't enough storage space for Jesus' words in the hearts of his hearers (John 8:37). At the start, in the world where his own people lived, they did not receive him (John 1:10-11); by the end that world is no longer able to store everything that could be written about him.

Before rushing on to something that we might consider to be more spiritual, let's pause to consider how much storage space we have. In the past 20 years our ability to store the written word has ballooned out of all recognition. Dusty libraries full of leather-bound tomes can easily be scanned onto a slice of silicon that you could pick up on a single finger. Is there really a problem with storage space?

The answer is that there is a limit because storage is only useful if you can retrieve what is stored. In the case of a library the time will still defeat us, for we can only read so many books an hour. John's challenge is how much of this news about Jesus will be stored up in our lives and through us in the world we live in. There are only so many hours in the day to read and meditate, there are only so many people we can talk to, there is only so much room in any world. This reinforces an earlier theme – the day is short and Jesus must be busy in it (John 9:4).

The idea of place as opposed to people, comes early on: 'He came to that which was his own, but his own did not receive him" (John 1:11). The reason this is tricky to translate is that it is a sort of wordplay – the same adjective is used in both cases as the word 'own' but in the first instance it is neuter, and so the commentators supply a range of ideas to fill in the blank – his own things, own possession, own land or even own home. The second time it is masculine, and the blank is much easier to fill in – his own people.

This confined sense of time and space feels like a play – Shakespeare's world as a stage, if you like – a world that Jesus came to, the stage on which this narrative was lived out, and where the people were who rejected him. Who were these people? To understand this, we need to delve into two more ways that John thinks about the world.

## A World of People

If the last reference in John is about place, the first clutch of references concerns people (John 1:9 and the verses that follow) – this is a world that is able to recognise and respond, although it did not do so at the time. So, his gospel is teeming with people. It is those people – all of them – whom God loved so much as to send his Son.

As we have noted, John uses a variety of techniques to convey the ever-present pressure of the world around Jesus. He describes different groups in general terms – the disciples, the crowd – and then he picks out a few so that we can hear authentic voices. The clouds of people who squat to listen or eat by the shore or who watch the miracles are often pencilled in very lightly. John does not tell us how many houses they overflowed from or how far they stretched before the bewildered eyes of the disciples. As we have noted, John's take on the spatial world is defocused, and by being sketchy about the crowds, he populates his world with individuals, real people, people like us.

Like his master before him, John cares about the world – not as an abstract mass, but as many, many individuals. John loves them too and he recognises that each one has a spiritual appetite and destiny. A crowd may be collectively starving or collectively curious, but the search for something more must be carried out for oneself. As a radiologist once told me when he was explaining how difficult it had been to move his department from X-ray film to digital imaging, 'You have to invest your own sweat equity'.

John knows that you do not have to journey alone, and he gives examples of networks and even a household (John 4:53) that support the encounter, individuals bringing other individuals. But you must decide for yourself, and John spends a lot of time looking for the 'sweat equity'.

As we have seen, some quickly recognise a satisfying conclusion to their quest and decide to follow in faith. Others are surprised, angry even, that their journey has brought them to this teacher and they rage against his ideas, his practices and against the man himself. The disciple who wanted, once upon a time, to call down fire from heaven upon an unreceptive crowd, now watches the world to see who will break ranks and come over to his side. He knows from long experience that some will, and he is deeply interested in the fate of those who will not – what is it that prevents them from deciding? He sees those for whom prolonged argument provides a path to redemption and those who are simply confirmed in their ways, for whom the heat of battle merely cures the resin of their first reaction into a hard, unbreakable decision. Lots of sweat but no equity in the end.

Over and over again, John tells us how Jesus came into this world to enlighten the people of the world (John 1:9), to save the people of the world (John 3:17), to provide a moral compass for the people of the world (John 8:12), to work among the people of the world (John 9:4), and to show them the glory of God (John 17:4). From time-to-time, even his opponents recognised that the world has gone after Jesus (John 12:19).

Without the world – the world of people – there would be no gospel. There would be no need of saving nor would there be any need of a saviour. Just as the birth of their first child conveys new titles on the parents – mother and father – so the existence of the world defines the way in which the eternal God becomes 'the Saviour of the world' (John 4:42). So, then, we have come full circle, the Word and the world, the need of the latter complementing the role of the former to fulfil the role that John's gospel is all about.

Clearly, it is more complicated than that, and I have no real idea what the interface between time and eternity feels like, but somehow it has room for the saved and their saviour, just as it accommodates the sender and the sent one.

We have spent a lot of time looking at people in John, and so we will move on and spend the rest of this chapter focusing on the third idea John has when he talks about the world. It also takes us back to the question about who the people were who rejected Jesus, and why.

## The World as a System

With the third usage, we open up a world for John that needs light against a latent darkness. He echoes those early verses of Genesis at the start of his great work, describing the struggle between the light and the dark, and this struggle spills over into his narrative about the world. In his gospel, 'the world' can also describe the thinking, the organisation, the politics, the culture and structures, even, that cannot find space for Jesus, and that lie in darkness as a result. This dark world, then, is a third meaning that John works with.

When it comes to the struggle between light and darkness, between Jesus and the world, in this sense, we find John at his most polar – he is describing opposites and there is no room for either to accommodate the other. We saw something of this in the most difficult aspects of the arguments between Jesus and the establishment (e.g. John 8:34-51, see chapter 12, *Jesus and the Rulers*).

The clash reaches a crescendo just ahead of the last meal that Jesus shared with his disciples – John reports that despite all the miracles, most of the people still won't believe. Why isn't the light destroying the darkness (John 12:35-37)?

To explain this, John appeals to Isaiah and uses a pair of quotations, the first from the famous Servant Song in Isaiah 53 (Isaiah 53:1; John 12:38). It is not hard to follow John's thinking as the narrative transitions from the local opposition to the tragedy foreseen by Isaiah. The crowd at the time may have struggled to make this connection. For one thing, if it tries to match the servant to the

Messiah, it has a picture of a suffering Messiah for which it is totally unprepared. With the meal approaching as he writes, there is a clear resonance that picks up his earlier theme of the Lamb of God and anticipates the connection with this passage from Isaiah, one that his contemporaries would all know well, one about wandering sheep and a lamb that is led to slaughter (John 1:29; Isaiah 53:6-7).

However, the struggle is more serious than that – they cannot see because they have been blinded. For this, John reaches back further into that ancient scroll and picks out a few verses describing the vision Isaiah has of God's glory – another of the great commissioning narratives of the Old Testament. Isaiah puts his hand up and agrees to go as a messenger, but the commission he receives is the most depressing in the Bible: he is to preach and be ignored until the people have gone into captivity (Isaiah 6:9-13; John 12:39-40). It is hard to read Isaiah's narrative without getting a sense that the message itself catalyses the deadening reaction, that people can get to a point where simply the sight of the light makes them wince and look away.

This would have been the most unpalatable of associations for Jesus' audience that day. They could understand that it had taken the great prophet Isaiah to preach against the sins of his day and yet to have been unable to elicit the repentance needed to save the land. They could understand that the idolatry and greed of generations had created a pressure that could only be released in captivity, but they were the children of those who had gone into captivity, who had learned the lessons of captivity. They were those who had re-inherited the land. Their predecessors had returned with a new focus on the scriptures, they were scrupulous in their weekly worship, in learning the scrolls off by heart, in tithing, and in teaching their children. How could the same thing be happening to the nation again? Can they have been blinded a second time and by what?

The same question arises in the debate the follows the healing of the blind man: Jesus says that the judgement he brings into the world opens some eyes and blinds others (John 9:39-41). Clearly the message that Jesus brings catalyses two very different reactions in his hearers. As my father sometimes said, the sun that softens wax hardens clay.

160

So, what is happening here? Let's dive into one of the sharpest arguments – Jesus tells his audience that they are ready to kill him because they have no room for his word (John 8:37). We have a similar metaphor reported in an earlier argument (John 5:37-38). The backdrop between light and darkness is also the divide between the Word and the world. His audience is from this world, Jesus is not (John 8:23). In John's writings, this is not a reaction between the new Christianity and the Judaism whence it came. When he is writing his letters to Christians in the wider world where there are all kinds of ideas, he is still warning against the world (1 John 2:15-17), and this time the things he warns against are clearly not particular religious practices, they are deeply embedded feelings – lust and pride.

## The Personal Edge of the World as a System

Jesus' message is a call to change, which forces everyone to make a decision either to cross over or to retrench. But because of the personal nature of the call, one cannot retrench without hostility.

If you can, in most arguments you want to focus on the issues rather than making it personal. Unless you are a particular type of politician, you usually want to get the voters to consider the issues, rather than simply to slag off members of the opposition. However, here there is no room to depersonalise things and take the heat out, because Jesus *is* the Word! Early on Jesus explains the predicament to his family – the world can't hate them but it can hate Jesus because he speaks against the evil in the world. In time, he tells his disciples that they will face the same hatred as their master – as they identify with him, they, too, will face the same reaction (John 7:7; 15:18-20).

The other key person in this usage of the term, 'world' is the 'prince of this world' (John 12:31; 14:30; 16:11). So, we have two systems headed up by two people, the world that follows its prince against the Word who obeys the Father and who is calling out followers from the world.

All else is battleground.

There is a sense of this when Jesus meets Pilate. I don't want to over read into the passage, but it seems to be that Jesus and Pilate have a much greater common understanding of delegated authority (John 18:33-19:16) than any other group whom John observes. Jesus is open with Pilate about how little real power he has (John 19:10-11), while Pilate soon latches onto the fact that Jesus' kingdom is from a different world, something about which he is initially relaxed, but about which he becomes terrified in time (John 19:7-8).

I think also, while not wishing to read too much into the narrative, that the distinction between the people and the power play allows John to be surprisingly understanding of the terrible decisions people make. The battleground is dappled – light and darkness – and people make their way out of the darkness or dig themselves deeper into the crevice in which they feel safe (John 3:20-21).

I find this perhaps the most difficult part of John's message. It is not possible to be friends all the time. One cannot depersonalise the debate and watch to see what will happen next or treat it merely as an interesting discussion. There is an edge.

## Crossing Over

The good news is that it is not the other way around, either. We are not compelled to oppose people just because of the tribe they belong to – however that tribe is defined. The story of the Samaritan village and their first ambassador – although they do not realise it – who comes to get water, sets the challenge in a racial and cultural setting, but Jesus and the woman have a very successful conversation. Any reading of John 4 shows that the racial and cultural tensions do not evaporate, but they do not define the discussion, either. In time and in a very different dimension, she moves from the world to follow the Word. Amazingly, she is not alone, for the village decides to come along too!

All the way through, John describes people who cross the border. Nicodemus and Joseph of Arimathea, while crossing from a different group, come over the same border. The blind man crosses into a new personal freedom and also across the same border. Many of the whisperers in the crowd take the step.

The unnerving thing for the establishment of Jesus' time was that the border was not defined in the way the rulers had hoped. For very rational reasons they wanted to define the border, nail down the criteria and make sure they stayed on the right side of it, but it wasn't that sort of border.

It wasn't that sort of border then and it isn't that sort of border now.

## Overcoming the World

One of the great rallying cries in John comes at the end of the discourse in that upper room. John provides no geographical pointers after the disciples gather for the last meal until they leave and cross the Kidron Valley. Some see the prayer in John 17 as taking place in Gethsemane, but you will have to consult a decent commentary to make up your own mind. As we have come to expect of John, he marks out his narrative with different staging posts, and so if you see John 17 as a longer extract of the prayer the synoptics report briefly in Gethsemane, the scene has changed. John signals a change with the great rallying cry that, although the world will surround them with trouble, he has overcome (John 16:33)!

This is the only time this particular word is used for 'overcome' in John's gospel. It is the word that goes with victory, and with sports outfits decorated with the famous tick. I had hoped that this was a partner to the clause at the start of John, the one about the darkness being unable to overcome the light (John 1:4), one echoing the other – but it is not. This is not an echo of something earlier.

However, there is a resonance to this verse in John's writing, but it is the other way around and the echo comes much later in John's life when he writes to Seven Churches. In each case it is the start of a promise to the individual who overcomes (Revelation 2:7, 11, 17, 26; 3:5, 12, 21), and in the final reference there is an eighth echo! There are seven churches but there are eight cases of overcoming, because there is a double-clap of victory at the end (Revelation 3:21) as Jesus reminds the churches that he, too, overcame and sat down with the Father. That isn't the end of the theme of victory, because the theme rumbles on through Revelation and this word comes back time and time again.

The struggle is difficult and real, but the victory is not in doubt. Within his lifetime he has watched the struggle of the world against his Master and has experienced the backlash against himself and those who followed on. In the end, however, it is victory, victory, victory.

## QUESTIONS

1 How does the tension between the Word and the world show up in your life?

2 To what extent does John's teaching on the world make you, as a Christian, confident and optimistic or cautious and suspicious of others. Outline a balanced position and explain how it could make you act differently in future.

3 Does John believe in personal evil? How about you?

4 In what ways is John's take on the world fundamentally different from his observations about the disciples, or the rulers, or the crowd?

5 To what extent have you experienced trouble in the world and victory over it?

6 Can you think of political or other regimes that have specifically aligned themselves against the Word? What has happened?

7 Is Christianity a cosmic faith?

# 15 | John on... Evidence

Believe me when I say that I am in the Father and the Father is in me; or at least believe on the evidence of the works themselves. (John 14:11)

But these are written that you may believe that Jesus is the Messiah, the Son of God, and that by believing you may have life in his name. (John 20:31)

John is clear that his gospel is a volume of evidence, but does he believe he can prove that Jesus Christ is the Son of God? Clearly not, because many of those he watches who encounter the evidence first hand, do not accept it. In fact, many of the Sanhedrin, who have a grandstand view, become more hostile as the evidence grows (e.g. John 11:47-53).

That said, John is clearly into testimony and witnesses. Even his reluctance to emerge from his own narrative accentuates his role as an observer, watching not just the evidence, but its impact on other people. He builds a multi-layered case, recognising that evidence only matters if it stacks up for the observer. Arguments that might appeal to a Pharisee will not work for a Samaritan outcast and, conversely, Pharisees simply cannot comprehend the sort of evidence it takes to persuade temple guards (John 7:45-49).

Having looked at the signs (chapter 5, *John on Signs*), let us return to consider what John is up to. We will start by considering evidence in its simplest form – marshalling the facts – and go on to discover that John is much more subtle in developing this theme. However, the signs provide a reference framework for John as he sets out to establish the evidence and we will need to return to them periodically as we follow John's ideas on what convinces what sort of person.

## Used in Evidence

Most of us link evidence to police investigations, usually in whodunits. My only experience of the courtroom was one summer around 'A'-level time, when a friend was considering law at university, so we went to watch a case. It was a long trial and I only saw a few days of it. As I recall, someone had been shot outside a nightclub, but the man on trial had meant to shoot someone else instead. Beneath the tawdry brutality, there was a neat little puzzle, but the law didn't grab me nor did it grab my friend, and I never found out how the trial finished.

Since a lot of the debate is of a legal nature (although not related to our idea of law), let us take the theme from there. The courtroom presents an unusual amalgam of experts and ordinary people seeking a fair solution. Even where evidence is clear, what convinces the judge may not score with the jury, so lawyers layer their lines of argument – if the alibi cannot be refuted, perhaps the prints on the lead pipe will win the day. A lawyer with just a single line of argument is usually a worried lawyer. So, watch with John to see who is being convinced:

- 'Now while he was in Jerusalem at the Passover Festival, many people saw the signs he was performing and believed in his name'. (John 2:23)

- 'Many of the Samaritans from that town believed in him because of the woman's testimony'. (John 4:39)

- 'Then the father realised that this was the exact time at which Jesus had said to him, "Your son will live." So he and all his household believed'. (John 4:53)

- 'They said, "Though John never performed a sign, all that John said about this man was true." And in that place many believed in Jesus'. (John 10:41, 42)

'Yet at the same time many even among the leaders believed in him'. (John 12:42)

Layering, but also logic. When my wife and I made our wills, our solicitor produced a draft for us to peruse. As I read it through, I realised how similar a will is to a computer program: if he dies first then this; if she dies first then that; if they both die at roughly the same time, then the other. Then he checked carefully that everything would be properly disposed of, whatever happened. No emotion, no texture or colour, just a set of statements strong enough to drive the machinery of inheritance, however tragic the events that might activate it. This is the great strength if the law – it works when we are too helpless, numb or angry to do things for ourselves.

At their best, then, lawyers are logical and objective. However, John's wry take is of lawyers more emotionally involved than they imagine, so that in the end their fury, rather than their argument, drives through the verdict in the trial before Pilate.

## Getting the Facts

Several years ago, I gave a talk to a conference of physics teachers called, *What's Physics Worth in the Big Wide World?* It compared perspectives from physics with those of other disciplines. Now while physics and the law share logical ideas, they establish facts differently. To scientists, there is a troubling angle to the idea that reality is established in a courtroom rather than a lab. What if you accidentally gather enough experts who assert that the world is flat? Would the world be flat for that case?

Of course, interrogating witnesses works in an important area where science fails, for science must be able to reproduce results – something Jesus refuses to do. He will perform a miracle to feed a crowd, but not on demand (John 6:1-13, 30, 31). The forensic laboratory is somewhere else where science and the law enjoy an uneasy relationship. Each year brings new capabilities, but also setbacks, with unsafe findings of trials based on expert evidence. Some certainties around Shaken Baby Syndrome evaporated, while those using DNA are having to be more careful in their calculations. Evidence that was incontrovertible a decade ago is highly contestable now. However, if the law's second-hand approach to reality through expert witnesses frustrates the scientist, it must frustrate the legal community that scientists cannot stick to the same story for long. One year babies should sleep on their backs to avoid cot death, another year they must be placed on their tummies or their sides.

John puts a surprising amount of effort into building a methodical case. Take the resurrection narrative, where John assembles his evidence as you would expect by establishing the end points. That Jesus was dead is attested first by the execution squad, which identifies that Jesus is dead and decides not to break his legs (John 19:33), a barbaric practice designed to stop those being crucified from pushing themselves up to breathe, thus hastening their end.

There is then some observation – a soldier stabs his spear deep inside and draws blood and water. I am not a medic, but I understand from Carson (*The Gospel According to John*) that there are a couple of modern explanations that fit – in either case, the victim is clearly dead. John understands the importance of these observations and underlines them carefully as eyewitness material (John 19:35). The need to secure the body through the highest channels, the careful process of tending to the body pending the proper burial, and the sheer amount of spice wound in (John 19:38-42) all add weight to the first point – Jesus was dead.

John establishes that Jesus was alive at the end in two ways – firstly through the empty tomb (John 20:1-9) and then through a series of encounters with people who then describe their meetings with Jesus. John's witnesses include Mary (John 20:11-18) and a group of the disciples minus Thomas (John 20:19-23); then a group with Thomas (John 20:26-29); and then seven disciples on the shores of the Sea of Galilee (John 20:1-14). Again, John has been counting, and he thinks that three is evidence enough.

However, John is not going to be able to give us technological proof. He has no time-stamping camera, nor sensors with telemetry to provide a continuous readout on temperature or chemical composition. In fact, we often forget just how young our era of instrumentation is. In *Galileo's Daughter*, Dava Sobel describes Galileo's attempts to measure the acceleration due to gravity, for instance, and you realise how crude his instrumentation was even a few hundred years ago. Without stopwatches to time falling objects, his genius lay in developing shallow ramps to roll things down, diluting the gravitational force to a point where his basic clocks could capture what was happening. Meanwhile, James Gleick's *Newton* reminds us how dependent people were on touching and tasting, and his description of Newton poking around behind his own eye is not for the squeamish! That people conjured such elegant maths from such limited apparatus is simply amazing.

Nonetheless, from a religious society that counts and weighs – days, offerings and incense – John provides us with numbers where he can, especially with arguments of causality – the father and son story analysed in Chapter 5 (*John on Signs*) shows how the timing of the healing son proved to be such a convincing element for his father and others (John 4:46-54).

He brings us as close to the action as he can, but he cannot convince people against their will. He has seen too many people walk away to believe that seeing a miracle will convince anyone. Some will find it convincing, others will not. Perhaps that is why he limits himself to just a few signs in his gospel. There is a question at the end on science and miracles for those who are interested.

## What Counts for Whom?

So much for science – what about behaviour? Do we believe someone would really behave like that? Could you engineer an effect like that? Would the critical evidence really sound like that over the phone? Would she really have composed that type of letter? Would you trust that person in spite of the circumstantial evidence?

Throughout the gospel, what happened, particularly at the end, was so far from what John and his fellow disciples were expecting that it constitutes one of the strongest evidential themes of the entire gospel. John tells us that Jesus tried to explain what was going to happen and that his disciples couldn't grasp it. For instance, John tells us that the disciples only realised afterwards the significance of Jesus' commitment to rebuild the temple in three days (John 2:19-22). The same is true on that first Palm Sunday (John 12:16). The two disciples do not realise that the tomb had to be empty (John 20:9), nor does Mary recognise the risen Christ at the tomb (John 20:14). Thomas is so convinced that his friend and master is gone forever, that he will not accept the evidence of his fellow disciples (John 20:19-29). His reaction when presented with a living, breathing, touchable Jesus, is the best of this type of evidence that John has to offer.

Judging things that happened in the heat of the moment or in an entirely alien environment is also a challenge for the courtroom. *The Today Programme* on BBC radio 4 this morning featured a judgement handed down against the Ministry of Defence over the actions of two peace-keeping soldiers. A criticism levelled against this judgement was that it was made in an environment unacceptably removed from the uncertain atmosphere of danger in which the original shootings took place. Indeed, it was possible that the ruling was based on the court assuming the soldiers to have had a different status to that which they believed themselves to have had at the time. The critic on the radio this morning was basically calling foul, unfair! The law may deliberate, but sometimes it needs to do better with the pressurised, fast-moving ambiguities of real life. Surprisingly, we find ourselves with some sympathy for Pilate, woken early and thrown back and forth between the frightening quietness of the accused and the vehemence of the crowd.

So what convinces you? Years ago, I visited the head of my old research group, whose research was into solar seismology – the way in which the sun wobbles and vibrates – and whose team was noted for their research trips to the cloud-free skies of Hawaii and Tenerife. He did not believe in God, but said that if there were a creator, he would expect to find a few things lying about the laboratory (and there were always things lying about his own lab) to enable us to make simple measurements. Surprisingly, for him, there was something – the moon. From earth, the sizes of sun and moon match almost exactly, a massive coincidence that has supported measurement, by way of eclipses, for thousands of years. Then, on the scale that astronomers use, the brightness of the moon lies about halfway between that of the sun and the brightest stars, providing a natural basis for a measurement scale. It didn't convince him... but it made him wonder.

I like this example, because it illustrates how personal this business of finding the right evidence can be. Clearly, John cannot interview people with all possible tastes and find something for everyone. Nor, as human knowledge develops and its values change, will he be able to anticipate what future generations will need. Despite this, John has catholic tastes in evidence and he weaves a variety of perspectives together for us – let's look.

## We Have Seen

So, let us return to the evidence of witnesses, what John and his fellow-disciples have seen (John 1:14) or what John the Baptist saw (John 1:29-34), through to the resurrection narratives, especially as Mary's testimony is echoed by the disciples to Thomas (John 19:35; 20:18, 25).

John's witnesses come in all shapes and sizes – so you have plenty of choice. Would you trust the cautiously conscientious Nicodemus (John 3; 7:50,51; 19:38-42), who is compelled by what he discovers to break ranks with the other Pharisees and his colleagues on the Sanhedrin or to go with Joseph to ask for Jesus' body? How about the Samaritan woman whom Jesus meets at the well (John 4:5-29)? I always think the locals are rather harsh when they tell the woman, 'We no longer believe just because of what you said; now we have heard for ourselves, and we know that this man really is the Saviour of the world' (John 4:42). She has little in common with Nicodemus – theologically, she and he are miles apart. Yet her appeal as a witness is more immediate, effective, and she persuades more people (John

4:39-41) – he cannot swing a majority on the Sanhedrin, while she convinces an entire city.

How about the disabled chap at the pool (John 5:2-15)? What sort of witness is this? Would you let him near the witness box as John has done? Yet, John has found a target for blessing who does not even care. He has hardly embellished his story – he is too preoccupied with his problems and too gauche to have done so.

At the other end of the disability spectrum is the man who was born blind (John 9), who enters the witness box with his street cred intact. He knows he was blind, that he met someone called Jesus who healed him, and that now he can see. Secure in his knowledge, he enrages his inquisitors by pointing out their deficiencies – 'Now that is remarkable! You don't know where he comes from' (John 9:30). So, would you trust man's evidence? Was he really healed? Was he right to believe and worship when he meets Jesus again (John 9:38)?

I love the evidence provided by the temple guards who were sent to arrest Jesus (John 7:32-52). When filleted by the authorities, they can only say, 'No one ever spoke the way this man does' (John 7:46). And there are lots more witnesses – some in full view, some in the shadows – and John gives them all a voice.

## Compelling Evidence

So what persuaded each of these witnesses? For me, the most difficult person to fathom is Nicodemus, whom we have studied at length (chapter 10, *John on One to One* and chapter 12, *John on the Rulers*). Something swings it for Nicodemus and he acts with courage beyond his caution. We do not have to guess what swung it for the Samaritan woman (John 4:4-42). Her lifestyle has added peer disapproval to an existence that was hard work anyway. Although she demonstrates that she can handle difficult concepts, reflection is a rare luxury for her. She must make up her mind about people quickly – and she does! This stranger knows all about her. That makes him a prophet in her book. His theology of worship stacks up and has room for Samaritans. When he claims to be the Messiah, she is convinced – she abandons her water jar and tears back to the village with the news.

It is not clear that the disabled man in John 5 really reaches any conclusions. The blind man is a different kettle of fish. He warms to Jesus initially because he has been healed. However, the opposition he faces from the authorities and their intimidating tactics (John 9:22) provide the catalyst that forces him to think it all through. In the end, it strengthens his resolve to stick to his guns. He starts out convinced that Jesus has done something special. Being forced to argue his corner turns out to be good for this chap, and he finds himself reasoning that God 'listens to the godly person who does his will. Nobody has ever heard of opening the eyes of a man born blind. If this man were not from God, he could do nothing' (John 9:31-33). Whether he would have reached this conclusion as incisively or quickly without the heat of battle is not clear. However, the battle leaves him ready to worship when next he meets Jesus (John 9:35-38). In this sense the argument has the opposite effect on him than it had on some of Jesus' other listeners.

## Colliding Worlds

I don't know about you, but the passages I find most difficult are the running arguments, particularly in John 5, 8 and 12 (John 6 and 7, too). The dislocation and fragmentation are more like an election narrative compiled for television than the extended discourse we might have expected from that era. However, John reminds us that the subplot is lethal – the authorities are out to kill Jesus. This is not about sticking to your guns at the press conference. The stakes are as high as any game of Russian roulette, and despite Jesus' expert footwork in the conflict, the debate proves fatal in the end.

I guess this is not the only reason why these passages are difficult. Even when the audience is sympathetic (for instance, with Nicodemus or the Samaritan woman), Jesus can be elliptic with his responses and mysterious in his descriptions. His replies are seeded with answers, but the answers are not always obvious. Those willing to listen and reflect will find them, but the casual or hostile listener is unlikely to get much out of them.

So, what are the key issues? As we have already noted, the authorities are predisposed against Jesus because he challenges their worldview, a revelation brought to them through Moses. We have already considered the relationship between Jesus and the writings, and noted the intense analysis that sprang up around the scriptures. This analysis presents a target for the New Testament writers. They contend that the nation has missed out on two key issues. First, it has lost sight of the fact that the scriptures were meant to broker a relationship with God, not to be an end in themselves. Paul writes, 'So the law was our guardian until Christ came that we might be justified by faith. Now that this faith has come, we are no longer under a guardian' (Galatians 3:24, 25). Second, the backward look has prevented people from looking forward to the very changes and developments that the law predicted. Jesus finds this last effect particularly frustrating: 'You study the Scriptures diligently because you think that in them you have eternal life. These are the very Scriptures that testify about me, yet you refuse to come to me to have life' (John 5:39, 40).

John does not seek to analyse this, although he is acutely aware of the difficulties it presents to those around at the time. If their legal framework is inviolate and if it comes from God, what are they to make of anyone who breaks the framework?

Let us return, for a minute to Dava Sobel's *Galileo's Daughter*, where one twist in the plot is that Galileo's daughter, Virginia, is forced to take the veil. As Sister Maria Celeste, she becomes part of a system that censures and oppresses her father over his views. Sister Maria Celeste comes through as a deeply thoughtful woman with a genuine and personal faith. Although she is never called upon to denounce him, she is still caught between love of her father and submission in her beliefs to the church authorities. For me, a moving piece is when she volunteers to undertake part of his punishment by reciting the penitential psalms weekly for three years.

The struggle between Galileo and the church is often used as an example of the clash between faith and science, but I now realise that it was more complicated. There was, for instance, a hefty element of power politics in play. The thing that struck me most was how heavily the church of the day had been influenced by factors outside of scripture. Its worldview was an amalgam of scripture plus ideas from elsewhere, including Aristotle. Although the charge was heresy, Galileo's crime was at least, if not much more, against Aristotle, and a massive element of his fight is with the mishmash of ideas inherited from Ancient Greece. In the text, Dava Sobel cites Galileo venting his frustration at the Aristotelians of his day, 'They wish never to raise their eyes from those pages – as if this great book of the universe had been written to be read by nobody but Aristotle, and his eyes had been destined to see for all posterity'. (You can also find the quotation readily online). It sounds a bit like an alternative religion and yet, so well had the establishment integrated what it understood from external sources with what it understood from scripture, that it was completely unaware of the difficulty. In a more modern context, *Reading Genesis after Darwin* explores such forces at play in our understanding of creation, while AN Wilson's recent biography, *Charles Darwin: Victorian Mythmaker*, finds yet another angle on the question of culture and science.

I believe that something similar has happened here. Around the Old Testament revelation has grown up an infrastructure of cultural ideas and regulations so that the authorities cannot see the difference between what was originally given and what has been added to it. Because of this, their conclusion is that anyone who challenges the framework – any part of the framework – cannot possibly be from God. Before we despise the Pharisees or the seventeenth century Roman Catholics, it is worth recalling how easily we accrete tradition and other miscellany into a framework of values that we claim has come from scripture alone.

## Prophetic Voices

Since John hopes to persuade some for whom this is a difficulty, he is careful to observe how many of the scriptures point to Jesus and what he did. For John, the scriptures provide a backdrop that helps him and the other disciples understand what Jesus is saying when he talks about rebuilding the temple in three days (John 2:22) or makes his call to the thirsty (John 7:37-39).

John has his little joke, too, at the expense of those who do not realise that Jesus was born in Bethlehem and who rule him out, not because they do not know their scriptures, but because they do not know their facts (John 7:40-43). Later on, he invokes Zechariah's joyful predictions about the coming king as a clear signpost to the events of Palm Sunday, although the disciples don't get it (John 12:14-16; Zechariah 9:9). Again, it is to scripture that Jesus appeals to defend himself against the charge of blasphemy (John 10:31-39; Psalm 82:6).

However, tying scripture to events that happen in Jesus' life becomes more common as we get towards the end of the gospel. For John and many of his early readers, the concept that key events were foreseen by the prophets and then fulfilled in Jesus' life was very powerful. So, as Jesus shares his Passover meal with a traitor, John notes that scripture has to be fulfilled, and recalls a snatch of a psalm:

> 'Even my close friend,
> > Someone I trusted,
> one who shared my bread,
> > has turned against me'.
> > (Psalm 41:9; compare John 13:18)

In particular, John presents in the details of the crucifixion evidence of prophetic eyes, straining ahead. He recalls scripture as he sees the soldiers dividing the Jesus' last possessions between them (John 19:23,24; Psalm 22:18). Psalm 22 is a remarkable psalm in anyone's book. Many years ago, we studied John's gospel in our home group, and closed the study of Jesus' death by reading this psalm. It is not clear what the exact circumstances experienced by the psalmist were, but the parallels with crucifixion are stunning. Laid out in the psalm are the excruciating pain of bones hauled out of joint (Psalm 22:14), bones that stand out (Psalm 22:17); the unbearable thirst (Psalm

22:15); the pierced hands and feet (Psalm 22:16); and the ultimate destiny in death (Psalm 22:15). Around are the crowds, some evil (Psalm 22:16), others gloating (Psalm 22:17), while others gamble (Psalm 22:18). Perhaps John's mind was still on this passage when he reports Jesus' awful thirst (John 19:28).

John recalls the Old Testament twice more in his record of the crucifixion itself – piecing together predictions that Jesus' bones would not be broken and that his body would be pierced (John 19:36, 37), the former being a prohibition on breaking the bones of the lamb sacrificed at Passover (Exodus 12:46; Numbers 9:12) and thus connecting back to his *Lamb of God* theme. The second quotation comes from the prophet Zechariah (Zechariah 12:10): 'They will look on me, the one they have pierced, and they will mourn for him as one mourns for an only child, and grieve bitterly for him as one grieves for a firstborn son'. For those of his era, the passage was clearly prophetic, as evinced by its recurring theme, 'On that day' (e.g. Zechariah 12:8, 9, 11; 13:1, 2). It provides evidence of divine foresight and also enables John to remind us how God the Father suffers as his heart is torn by the savage scene unfolding before us. These passages may not prove decisive for us, but there were people at the time for whom this would have made a compelling case.

By the time he gets to the empty tomb (John 20:8-9), John clearly understands that the whole thrust of the Old Testament was that the Messiah had to come, die and rise again. This theme underpins Luke's story about the two dejected followers who have yet to hear about the resurrection, making their dreary way to Emmaus, when Jesus meets up with them. In the end, Jesus gets a little exasperated with their lack of understanding that this was how it had to be. 'He said to them, "How foolish you are, and how slow of heart to believe all that the prophets have spoken! Did not the Christ have to suffer these things and then enter his glory?" And beginning with Moses and all the Prophets, he explained to them what was said in all the Scriptures concerning himself' (Luke 24:25-27). We can see how the disciples started to piece this puzzle together by looking at Peter's first sermon (Acts 2:14-39) and tracking back through scripture. I will leave that as an exercise for you with a question at the end.

## Reflection

So how does this stack up for you? Clearly it did not convince everyone at the time, but for those whom it did convince, it was like a light going on in their heads. Perhaps they were so programmed for a triumphant Messiah who would rid them of their enemies and create a kingdom on earth, that they had discarded those other pieces of the jigsaw about death and humiliation. However, once they see it all fitting together, they can only slap their foreheads and say, 'Of course!'

I wonder if you remember those autostereograms that were a minor rage in the '90s? They appeared in weekend supplements and someone even sent me one as a Christmas card. People would stare into what looked like an amorphous collection of small shapes and say, 'No… no… nothing. Wait a minute, it's the Sydney Opera House!' Until you saw it for yourself, you thought this was a conspiracy. The thing about autostereograms was that you couldn't just see a bit. You either saw the whole or you didn't. Some people never got it.

All evidence of signs, of discussion, of prophecy beforehand, or of the believability of witnesses pale into insignificance next to the great crisis event near the end of John's gospel, and we will finish there.

# QUESTIONS

1 How many lines of argument does Luke report Jesus as using when it came to debate about the Sabbath? Try Luke 6:1-5; 6:6-11; 13:10-17 and 14:1-6. How might we apply this in our lives?

2 Go through John and pick out the references the author makes to passages in the scriptures – most modern Bibles will have them in a column down the middle of the page or at the bottom. Now group them into themes, such as direct prophecies or explanatory references, that would have furnished evidence for the early readers. How many of those do you find convincing? Describe why you find the others less convincing?

3 Starting with Peter's sermon (Acts 2:14-41) and tracking back through the passages he refers to, describe how the early Christians connected their legacy of scripture with their experience of salvation through Jesus and new life in the Spirit.

4 Does the fact that John has counted the water jars at the wedding of Cana make his narrative more convincing or not. If so, why? If not, why not?

5 What arguments might you marshal if a friend who was well-informed in science and technology complained that he or she could not accept John's narrative because of all the miracles? Which arguments would you drop, strengthen or add, if your friend was a research scientist?

6 Why types of evidence that John furnishes most appeal to you – describe them and explain why they appeal. Do you prefer the detail – each piece of evidence and the types of evidence – or the whole picture?

7 How does John answer Pilate's question, 'What is Truth?' (John 18:38).

# 16 | EPILOGUE

No one ever spoke the way this man does (John 7:46)

The bewildered guards facing the wrath of their employers have to explain why they did not arrest Jesus as ordered. Better minds and the political consensus are heavily stacked up against them, but the guards sense from somewhere that their orders cannot possibly have been for the best. In a moment, John has captured the essence of all he set out to achieve – he has laid bare the point of decision at the heart of any encounter with Jesus. It is not just what you believe about Jesus that matters – it also matters what you are going to do about it. The scene has been chosen with care and the atmosphere swirls with uncertainty, belligerence and the total absence of a fence to sit on. The guards may not be as good at reasoning as their bosses, but might their reasons be better? Sooner or later, John wants to bring us to the same point – we cannot avoid the question and he would rather we did not defer an answer: what are we going to do?

John has something unbelievable to communicate, so unbelievable that he really did not have a clue what was going on at the time. From chapter 13 to chapter 20, roughly a third of his gospel, John is describing the events of just a few days. What comes before points towards it, what comes afterwards points back. All John's skill in presenting evidence is marshalled behind this incredible sequence of events – rising conflict, death, resurrection, faith and everlasting life.

So what do you make of John's gospel? Has he fulfilled the challenge he set himself? Is there a line of evidence that convinces you? Does the integrated picture make a convincing whole?

If you watch with John, you cannot look at the evidence and remain unchanged. For some, often those in leadership, the unfolding evidence has hardened their position. However neutral or even sceptical they were at the start, all the arguing and watching has moved them firstly to a position of not believing, and on to a position so fiercely opposed to Jesus that they are quite prepared to sacrifice him to retain the status quo. John's coverage focuses heavily on the trial before Pilate, where the tension between Pilate and the leadership boils down to the question of whether he is going to rubber-stamp their decision or explore the evidence for himself. Even Jesus pushes him on this one.

In the end, Pilate decides that this is not about evidence but politics. The depth of ill will between the governor and the governed reverberates well after the verdict has been implemented. And he is partly right – it was never just about the evidence but about what you were going to do with it and about it.

Matthew's Pilate washes his hands (Matthew 27:24), while John's Pilate utters something profound and marches back out to the accusing crowd, but in neither case can he really walk away. It is the same for everyone else whom John has been watching. Everyone in John's story had a history that went on afterwards – some happily, some less so – and since John was so young when he observed these people and so old when he dies, presumably most of their lives were over by the time he describes their encounters to us. They met Jesus, they saw what he did, they listened to what he said, they weighed the arguments and made or deferred their decisions.

As we have noted, John is not simply interested in whether we get over the bar, whether we achieve a working faith, whether we believe. John is desperate that we should get to know this Jesus as he knew him, to enjoy his presence and to step out into the life in all its fullness. This is not a second decision, it is an on-going decision – and for most people who read this book, it is probably the more relevant decision.

John does not tell us what happened to all the people who met Jesus. Some lives were lived in public and we can find out how they fared from other sources. Some became known within the newly born Christian community, and again, we know something about some of them through the writings that circulated amongst that community. Most, we never meet again.

Now John makes it possible for us to meet Jesus, to listen to him and see what he did, to meet the Father and to get to know the Spirit, to sense the heartbeat that drove those encounters first time around. He wants you (and me!) to keep deciding.

We cannot walk away, either. John's first aim is that we should come to faith – he hopes the evidence persuades us – you and me. And then he hopes that each one of us will do something about it by becoming a disciple and making Jesus' habits our own. Which brings us nicely to the last thing Jesus says in John (John 21:22): 'Follow me!'

## Reading List

SC Barton, D Wilkinson, *Reading Genesis after Darwin*, Oxford University Press, 2009

DA Carson, *The Gospel According to John*, IVP, 1991

CR Nicholl, *The Great Christmas Comet*, Crossway Books, 2015

D Sobel, *Galileo's Daughter*, HarperCollins, 1999

RD Williams, *Christ on Trial*, Harper Collins Religious, 2000

AN Wilson, *Charles Darwin: Victorian Mythmaker*, John Murray, 2017

# ABOUT THE AUTHOR

Terry Young is an amateur who started writing in the late '90s when he worked in a research centre outside Chelmsford and was part of the leadership team at Tile Kiln, a local, independent, evangelical church. His first three books, *Jake: Just Learn to Worship*, *After the Fishermen* and *Going Global*, were published by Partnership and Paternoster Press. More recently, he has started writing again, when Words by Faith published *Making Sense of Romans When You Read it for Yourself* in 2016

His day job as an academic involves teaching project management, and particularly in finding new ways to deliver courses and engage students using emerging technologies. However, he is on sabbatical for the academic year 2017/18. His research focuses on health services: how they are organised and, again, how new technology can make an impact in yielding better care under constrained budgets.

Terry and Dani live in Datchet and worship at a Slough Baptist Church nearby. Their home is emptying, and the family spreads as far south as Hampshire and as far north as Durham. Meanwhile, their first grandchild arrived in 2017.

# SUBJECT INDEX

Abraham   67, 94

Acting on God's will   107, 109

Affluence   95

Andrew   45, 82, 122, 124, 147

Angels   83, 90

Aristotelianism   177

Atheism   49

Authors (other) on John   4

Authorship of John   5

Baptism   48

Barriers to belief   49

Bartholomew — see Nathanael

Belief   31, 43ff

Believers as individuals   157-8

Believers, relations among   131

Believers, response to Jesus   142, 183, 184

Bethesda, healing of man at   57

Bethlehem   178

Betrayal of Jesus   178

Bible Hub   4, 10, 26, 35, 81

Bible study   2, 3, 4

Blind man   24, 25, 45, 60, 81, 91, 96, 149, 160, 162, 174, 175

Body and blood of Jesus   72

Bread of life   82

Bread, Jesus' identification with   70-72, 74

Burial of Jesus   139

Caesar   140

Caiaphas   141, 143

Cana, wedding at   55, 92, 101-103, 181

Chief priests   62

Childbirth   83

Children of God   27

Christ, the   8

Christian values   94-95

Christmas   33

Conversation as Christian witness   106-107, 117

Conversations, Jesus'   112-115

Conversion, variety of reasons for   153, 154

Converts, as distinct from disciples   48

Crisis, as spur to faith   149-151, 154

Crowd's motivation to follow Jesus   147

Crowds in the gospels   145ff

Crucifixion   83, 139, 151

Crucifixion, prefigured in OT   178, 179

Darkness   91, 93

Death of Jesus   106, 170

Death, our preparation for   107, 109

Development of faith   50, 52

Disciples, John's view of   121ff

Divorce   95

Emmaus   179

Empty tomb   172, 179

Eucharistic belief, Catholic & Protestant   72

Evangelism   48

Evidence, gospel as   167ff

Evidence, miracles as   64

Evidence, variety of in John   168-9,
    171-2, 174
Evil   91, 93, 161, 165
Ezekiel   80, 86
Ezra   11
Faith as opposition to the world   162
Faith of the disciples   46-47
Faith, as experienced now   47-48,
Faith, disciples' development in   34
Faith, life of   44
Faith, variety of ways of coming to
    153
Family of Jesus   148
Family relationships   95
Father, relation with Jesus   10, 20ff
Father, Son, Spirit —relationship
    between   37, 39
Fatherhood of God   19ff, 44
Fish, miraculous haul of   63
Following Jesus   50
Fruit of the vine   86
Galileo controversy   177
Gamaliel   135
Gate   74
Gethsemane   74-75, 92, 163
Giving   95
Glory as suffering   82-83
Glory of God   158
Glory passed on   85-87
Glory, in relation to 'the hour'   102
Glory, two types in John   79ff
God as Father   19ff
God the Father, suffering of   179
God, presence to believers   69-70
God, self-disclosure   76
Good and evil   93
Gospel, how to spread now   117, 119,
    120
Grace   81, 87
Happiness   95
Herod   136, 140, 148
Hour, the   99ff
Hour, the in relation to glory   102

'I am' statements   67ff
Idolatry   23
Incarnation   61
Internet & bible study   3, 4
Isaiah   23, 80, 81-82, 159, 160
Israel, history and the Law   11
Israelites   67ff, 71
James   122ff
Jesus   8, 10
Jesus as teacher   96
Jesus as way to the Father   95
Jesus, arguments about identity of
    138, 139
Jesus, as described by John   112
Jesus, as means of salvation   94
Jesus, as the Word   10, 12
Jesus, believers' relation with   130,
    183, 184
Jesus, betrayal of   178
Jesus, birth of   178
Jesus, criticism of Jewish leaders   137
Jesus, difference from Moses   20
Jesus, disciples' understanding of
    129, 131
Jesus, divinity of   70, 77, 94
Jesus, does Father's work   24
Jesus, King of the Jews   10
Jesus, message of accepted and reject-
    ed   160, 161
Jesus, mission of   158
Jesus, own awareness of destiny   103-
    104, 107, 109
Jesus, power of   76
Jesus, relation to Moses   69, 71, 75-76
Jesus, relation to women   122
Jesus, relation with Father   10, 20ff
Jesus, teaching about himself   175
Jesus, view of John the Baptist   137
Jesus: prophet or Messiah?   147, 148
Jesus' challenge to Jewish teaching
    176
Jewish leadership   184
Jewish teaching, challenged by Jesus

176, 177
Jewish-Roman relations   135
Jews   133ff
Jews and Samaritans   111
Jews, children of Israel   67
Jews, relation with God   61
John (as disciple)   45, 122ff, 126
John the Baptist   8, 34, 40, 45, 84, 90,
    125, 126, 133, 135, 136ff, 145, 146,
    147, 173
Joseph of Arimathea   24, 138-139,
    141, 149, 150, 162, 173
Judas Iscariot   89, 92, 93, 97, 123ff,
    127ff, 141
Judas (Thaddeus)   123ff
Judgement   13
Kidron Valley   163
King of the Jews   141
Kingdom, nature of   162
Knowing God   20
Knowing Jesus, through John   183-
    185
Knowledge, light of   96
Lamb of God   106, 136, 160, 179
Last Supper   38, 72, 75, 126, 159, 163,
    178
Law, Jewish   11, 67ff, 176
Lazarus   8, 46, 61-62, 73, 75, 81, 84,
    91, 113-114, 153
Leadership   143
Levites   8, 11, 133
Life in the Spirit   36
Life, eternal   36, 44
Life, light and   91-92, 97
Light and darkness   89ff, 159, 162,
    163
Light and morality   93, 95
Light of knowledge   96
Light of the world   72-73, 77, 97
Light, glory as   80ff
Loaves and fishes miracle   58, 126
Love, God's for the world   28
Love, of Father for Son   25

Luke   31, 32, 33, 60, 90, 92, 112, 114,
    122, 129, 135, 179, 181
Man healed at Bethesda   117, 174,
    175
Mark   33, 56, 89, 90, 92, 112
Martha and Mary   8, 48, 53, 62, 101,
    113-114, 122
Mary and Joseph   90
Mary Magdalene   84, 89, 112-113,
    122, 152, 170, 172, 173
Mary mother of Jesus   55, 99, 103,
    105, 122
Matthew   31, 33, 59, 89, 92, 112
Messiah   34, 179
Messiah, evidence of Jesus as   167ff
Messiah, suffering   160
Miracles, see Signs
Morality, light and   93, 94, 95
Moses   11, 63, 65, 67ff, 71, 75, 76, 80,
    81, 94, 176
Moses, difference from Jesus   20
Moses, law of   49
Nambiguara tribe   71
Nathanael (Bartholomew)   45, 123ff,
    148
Nicodemus   24, 27, 35, 36, 83, 91-94,
    96, 114-116, 138-139, 141, 149, 50,
    162, 174, 175, 173
Night and day imagery   92, 97
NIV (New International Version)
    133-4
Old Testament prophecy fulfilled
    178, 179
Other faiths & worldviews   49
Overcoming through faith   163
Palm Sunday   172, 178
Passion of Jesus   105
Passover   179
Patmos   84
Paul   17, 60, 176
Peter   31, 45, 50, 83, 87, 106, 128,
    131, 148, 150, 179, 181
Pharisees   7, 11, 36, 60, 96, 98, 133,

134, 167, 173, 177

Philip   45, 82, 123ff, 126, 131, 147

Pilate   10, 117, 135, 140-142, 151, 162, 169, 172, 181, 184

Planning for the hour   105

Power of Jesus   162

Power, of the Word   14

Prayer, to understand God's will   107

Priests (Jewish)   133, 134

Prince of this world   161

Prologue   90

Prophecies about Jesus   178, 179

Rabboni   112

Race and culture   162

Recognising Jesus   63, 65

Relationship with Jesus   64

Resurrection of Jesus   61, 105, 152

Resurrection, appearance after   129

Resurrection, witness evidence   170, 171-2

Revelation, of Father in Jesus   22

Revivals, evangelical   149

Roman authorities   135

Roman Catholics   177

Routes to God   49

Royal official (& son)   56, 139, 153, 171

Rulers, Jewish   133ff

Sabbath   11, 49, 57-58, 60, 181

Sadducees   36, 60, 134

Samaritan woman   35, 45, 111, 114-116, 162, 173-175

Samaritans   133, 148, 167

Sanhedrin   134, 167, 173

Satan   127

Saviour of the world   158

Science and religion   177, 181

Scripture, in Judaism   11

Seed, death of   83

Sending (communications)   8, 9

Sending, of Jesus by the Father   49

Sending, of the disciples   87

Seven churches (in Revelation)   163

Shepherd, Good   74

Shepherd/sheep faith analogy   50, 51, 74, 160

Sign, Jesus as   75

Signs   23, 47, 49, 55ff, 159, 167, 171

Simon (see also Peter)   45, 122

Sin (lust and pride)   161

Solomon   80

Son of God, evidence for   167

Son of Man   82

Spirit, disciples' relation with   38, 40

Spirit, God as   35

Spirit, Holy   31ff, 84, 95, 101, 102

Spirit, sent by the Father   39, 40

Suffering, glory and   83

Suffering, understanding of   88

Synoptic gospels   27, 33, 92, 145,163

Tabernacles, feast of   73, 148

Temple guards   148-9, 167, 174, 183

Temple, Jerusalem   134, 135

Temple, rebuild in three days   172, 178

Ten Commandments   80

Thomas   31, 70, 123ff, 141, 172-3

Time, John's use of   101ff

Transfiguration   83

Trinity   34, 37

'Truly, truly' sayings   67

Truth   81, 87, 143

Truth, light and   91-92, 97

Twelve, the   122ff, 126-127

Victory of Christ   163-4

Vine, the   73, 86

Voices, sound of in John   84

Walking on the water   59

War, glory and   88

Water of life   77

Way, the   73

Witness, light and   90, 92, 97

Witnesses to the Resurrection   173

Witnessing   98

Women at the crucifixion   152

Women, Jesus' relation to   122

Word, as too large for the world   156
Word, contrast with world   161, 165
Word, Jesus as   7ff, 33
Work, of Christians   27
Work, of Father and Son   25
World (also cosmos)   155ff, 165
World as object of Jesus' mission   158
World as overcome by Jesus   163
World as people   157ff
World as physical space   155ff
World as system/structures   159ff
World, God's love for   26
Zacchaeus   145
Zechariah   178

# Scripture Index

1 John 2:15-17   161
1 John 4:14   49
1 Kings 8:12   80
1 Peter 3:15   106
1 Peter 4:12-19   83
1 Timothy 4:2   91
2 Chronicles 6:1   80
2 Chronicles 7:1-3   80
2 Corinthians   2
2 Corinthians 3:6   17
2 Timothy 2:15   4
2 Timothy 2:19   48
Acts 1:14-15   122
Acts 2:1-4   32
Acts 2:14-39   180
Acts 2:14-41   181
Acts 3:1-10   58
Acts 5:34-39   135
Acts 12:1-2   123
Acts 12:18-19   148
Acts 23:1-10   60
Acts 23:8   60
Deuteronomy   88
Deuteronomy 28:15-68   11
Deuteronomy 32:39   76
Ecclesiastes 9:10   97
Exodus   88
Exodus 3:1-17   68
Exodus 3:1-4:17   76
Exodus 3:13   68
Exodus 3:14   68, 76
Exodus 3:16   68
Exodus 12:46   179

Exodus 13:20-21   72
Exodus 13:21-22   69
Exodus 16   71
Exodus 16:4-32   71
Exodus 17   71
Exodus 17:1-7   71
Exodus 33:18-2   80
Exodus 34   80
Ezekiel 15:1-8   86
Galatians 3:24, 25   176
Genesis   12
Isaiah 6   88
Isaiah 6:9-13   160
Isaiah 6:10   82
Isaiah 40:25   23
Isaiah 44:14-20   23
Isaiah 48:12   76
Isaiah 51:12   76
Isaiah 53   88
Isaiah 53:1   159
Isaiah 53:6-7   160
Isaiah 53:11   83
John 1   92
John 1:1   7
John 1:4   72, 91, 163
John 1:7   137
John 1:9   91, 157, 158
John 1:10-11   90, 156
John 1:11   26, 156
John 1:12   44
John 1:12-13   27
John 1:14   12, 81, 87, 173
John 1:17   69, 81

John 1:17-18   20
John 1:18   29
John 1:19   8, 133
John 1:19-28   136, 146, 134
John 1:24   133
John 1:29   106, 160, 136
John 1:29-34   173
John 1:32-34   34, 84
John 1:35-42   123
John 1:35-51   45
John 1:40   123
John 1:40-51   127
John 1:41, 45   148
John 1:43   45
John 1:43, 45   123
John 1:45-51   125
John 1:50   27
John 1:50-51   46
John 2:1   92
John 2:1-11   47, 55, 81, 102
John 2:3   55
John 2:4   99
John 2:6   55, 133
John 2:8-10   56
John 2:9   56
John 2:11   43, 46, 81
John 2:12-17   29
John 2:18   134
John 2:19-22   172
John 2:22   46, 178
John 2:23   49, 153, 168
John 3   35, 114, 173
John 3:1-21   27
John 3:2   92, 96
John 3:8   35
John 3:11   96
John 3:13-15   83
John 3:16   26, 44
John 3:16-17   155
John 3:16-21   27
John 3:17   13, 158
John 3:17-18   93
John 3:19-21   93

John 3:20   91
John 3:20-21   162
John 3:28   8
John 3:35   25
John 3:36   44
John 4   35, 77, 114, 133, 162
John 4:1-42   44
John 4:4-42   24, 174
John 4:5-29   173
John 4:9   111
John 4:13-15   147
John 4:14   44
John 4:21-24   35
John 4:26   69
John 4:29   148
John 4:39   45
John 4:39   168
John 4:39-41   173
John 4:41   49
John 4:42   158, 173
John 4:43-54   24, 53
John 4:46-53   139
John 4:46-54   56, 171
John 4:48   55
John 4:53   158, 168
John 5   10, 117, 175
John 5-12   12
John 5:1-15   24, 53
John 5:2-15   57, 174
John 5:8-16   49
John 5:16-18   11
John 5:16-27   24
John 5:17   25, 97
John 5:19b   10
John 5:22   13
John 5:24   47, 93
John 5:25   15
John 5:26   37
John 5:33-35   146
John 5:33-36   137
John 5:35   147
John 5:37-38   161
John 5:39-40   11, 176

John 5:45   11
John 6   10, 36, 73, 70, 175
John 6:1-13   58, 169
John 6:1-15   47
John 6:2-5   146
John 6:5-7   126
John 6:5-9   126
John 6:7   126
John 6:7-8   124
John 6:9   59
John 6:10   59
John 6:13   59
John 6:14   59
John 6:16-21   59
John 6:17   101
John 6:19   59
John 6:20   69
John 6:21   59
John 6:25-27   147
John 6:26   59, 145
John 6:27   147
John 6:30-31   169
John 6:31-33   71
John 6:35   70
John 6:38-39   10
John 6:41   70
John 6:42   22
John 6:43-59   82
John 6:48   70
John 6:51   70
John 6:52   134
John 6:53   71
John 6:53-65   36
John 6:57   44
John 6:63   37
John 6:65   36
John 6:66   50
John 6:67-70   123
John 6:68   36
John 6:69   46
John 6:70-71   93, 127
John 6:71   123
John 7   10, 73, 77, 104, 175

John 7:6   109
John 7:6-8   101
John 7:7   161
John 7:12   148
John 7:14   101
John 7:14-52   148
John 7:19   137
John 7:19, 25   137
John 7:30   99, 103
John 7:30-31   153
John 7:31   148
John 7:32   8
John 7:32-52   174
John 7:32-45   134
John 7:37   84, 101
John 7:37-39   71, 138, 178
John 7:37-44   148
John 7:39   36, 102
John 7:40-42   148
John 7:40-43   178
John 7:45-49   167
John 7:45-52   93, 134, 148
John 7:46   183
John 7:46   174
John 7:47-49   136
John 7:48   138
John 7:48-49   133
John 7:50   92
John 7:50-51   139, 173
John 7:50-53   115
John 7:52   137
John 7:53-8:11   120, 122
John 8   10, 73, 77, 81, 94, 104, 175
John 8:1-11   77
John 8:12   36, 72, 77, 89, 158
John 8:12-30   22
John 8:15-16   13
John 8:16, 29   38
John 8:19   22
John 8:20   99, 103
John 8:22   134
John 8:23   143, 161
John 8:23-29   138

John 8:24   44
John 8:24, 28   69
John 8:28   83
John 8:30   153
John 8:31   49
John 8:32   91
John 8:34-51   159
John 8:37   156, 161
John 8:37-40   137
John 8:39-44   24
John 8:42-47   23, 137
John 8:48   133
John 8:50, 54   81
John 8:54   79
John 8:55   24
John 8:58   67
John 9   24, 44, 81, 91, 96, 174
John 9:1-4   60, 97
John 9:3   25, 81
John 9:4   156
John 9:5   97
John 9:7   8
John 9:8-9   60
John 9:12   60
John 9:16   11, 61
John 9:17   148
John 9:20-23   60
John 9:22   175
John 9:24   81
John 9:30   174
John 9:31-33   175
John 9:35-38   175
John 9:38   45, 174
John 9:39-41   160
John 10   10, 50, 74
John 10:7-9   74
John 10:9   70
John 10:10   36, 44, 95, 98
John 10:11   70
John 10:11, 14   74
John 10:16   74
John 10:27-28   50
John 10:27-30   48

John 10:31-39   178
John 10:37-38   46
John 10:40-42   146
John 10:41-42   168
John 10:42   49
John 11   53, 82, 113, 114
John 11:1-44   61
John 11:3   8
John 11:4   81
John 11:6   62
John 11:15   46
John 11:16   123
John 11:20-28   113
John 11:21-26   73
John 11:21-32   62
John 11:25   74
John 11:30   101
John 11:32-34   113
John 11:33   62
John 11:35   62, 113
John 11:39   62
John 11:41-42   113
John 11:43   62, 84
John 11:45   49, 62, 153
John 11:45-50   12
John 11:45-53   134
John 11:47-48   135
John 11:47-53   167
John 11:47b–48a   62
John 11:49-53   138, 143
John 12   10, 81, 82, 94, 175
John 12:2-9   62
John 12:4-6   127
John 12:6   93
John 12:10   62, 137
John 12:11   153
John 12:14-16   178
John 12:16   172
John 12:19   82, 158
John 12:20-21   127
John 12:20-22   124
John 12:20-33   102
John 12:23-26   83

John 12:23-28   99
John 12:23-29   82
John 12:23-33   104
John 12:23-27   100
John 12:27   82
John 12:27-28   26, 99
John 12:27-29   84
John 12:31   161
John 12:32-33   83
John 12:35-37   159
John 12:37-41   82
John 12:38   159
John 12:39-40   160
John 12:40   82
John 12:42   49, 138, 169
John 12:43   24
John 12:44-50   137
John 12:45   10
John 12:47   13
John 12:47b-48   13
John 13-16   38, 105
John 13:2   93, 127
John 13:7   50
John 13:18   178
John 13:19   46, 69
John 13:22-24   128
John 13:23   123
John 13:26-30   93, 127
John 13:30   89, 92, 97
John 14   4
John 14:6   49, 73, 74, 94, 95, 138
John 14:8   126
John 14:8-14   21
John 14:9   10
John 14:9-11   46
John 14:9-14   40
John 14:11   167
John 14:12   41
John 14:12   27
John 14:14-21   38
John 14:15-17   39
John 14:16-17   37
John 14:22   123

John 14:24   10
John 14:29   46
John 14:30   161
John 15   4
John 15:1   70
John 15:1-8   73, 86
John 15:1-17   50
John 15:7   27
John 15:8   85
John 15:18-20   161
John 15:26   37
John 16:5-11   37
John 16:8   95
John 16:11   161
John 16:12   2
John 16:17-19   63
John 16:20-22   83
John 16:23-28   26
John 16:31   53
John 16:32   25
John 16:32   38
John 16:33   163
John 17   25, 88, 102, 163
John 17:1   99
John 17:1-5   86, 104
John 17:3   96
John 17:4   158
John 17:20   86
John 18   10
John 18:1-12   92
John 18:2-7   128
John 18:2-11   76
John 18:5, 6, 8   69, 75
John 18:15   135
John 18:15-18   150
John 18:18   129
John 18:20-21   146
John 18:25-27   150
John 18:29-31   141
John 18:33   162
John 18:38   117, 120, 143, 181
John 19   103
John 19:7-8   162

John 19:10-11  162
John 19:12-16  139
John 19:16  162
John 19:16b-37  106
John 19:19  10
John 19:19-22  141
John 19:23-24  178
John 19:25  122, 152
John 19:25-27  105
John 19:28  105, 179
John 19:33  170
John 19:34  152
John 19:35  170, 173
John 19:36, 37  179
John 19:38-42  24, 93, 115, 149, 139, 170, 173
John 19:39  92
John 20  103, 114
John 20:1  89, 97
John 20:1-9  170
John 20:1-14  170
John 20:1-18  152
John 20:3-9  47
John 20:8  46
John 20:8-9  179
John 20:9  172
John 20:11-13  84
John 20:11-18  112, 170
John 20:14  172
John 20:17  19, 44
John 20:18  173
John 20:19-23  170
John 20:19-29  172
John 20:21  16, 27
John 20:21,22  87
John 20:22  31
John 20:24  123
John 20:25  173
John 20:26-29  170
John 20:28  46
John 20:31  44, 167
John 21  34
John 21:1-12  63

John 21:2  123
John 21:7-20  123
John 21:9  129
John 21:12  63, 129
John 21:18-19  106
John 21:19  87
John 21:21  121
John 21:22  50, 185
John 21:24  122
John 21:25  7, 156
Jude  9
Leviticus  88
Luke 1  136
Luke 1:35-45  34
Luke 1:46-79  114
Luke 1:80  136
Luke 3:1-18  136
Luke 3:19-20  136
Luke 5:1-11  129
Luke 6:1-5  181
Luke 6:12-16  131
Luke 6:14  123
Luke 6:16  123
Luke 6:36  19
Luke 6:6-11  181
Luke 9:51-56  123
Luke 11:2  19
Luke 13:1  135
Luke 13:10-17  181
Luke 14:1-6  181
Luke 17:5-6  50
Luke 22:47-54  92
Luke 23:44,45  92
Luke 23:47  152
Luke 23:50-51  139
Luke 24:25-27  179
Mark 1:6  136
Mark 1:29-31  56
Mark 3:16-19  131
Mark 3:17  122
Mark 3:18  123
Mark 3:18  123
Mark 6:17-29  136

Mark 7:24-30   45
Mark 10:46-52   45
Mark 11:26   19
Mark 14:43-50   92
Mark 15:33   92
Mark 15:43   139
Matthew 3:4   136
Matthew 6:14-15   19
Matthew 6:9   19
Matthew 9:27-31   45
Matthew 10:2-4   131
Matthew 10:3   123
Matthew 14:3-12   136
Matthew 14:22-34   59
Matthew 20:20-23   123
Matthew 26:47-56   92
Matthew 27:24   184
Matthew 27:45   92
Matthew 27:54   152
Nehemiah 8:7,8   11
Numbers   88
Numbers 9:12   179
Numbers 21:4-9   83
Philippians 1:6   43
Psalm 147:19-20   68
Psalm 22   178
Psalm 22:14   178
Psalm 22:15   178
Psalm 22:15   179
Psalm 22:16   179
Psalm 22:17   178
Psalm 22:17   179
Psalm 22:18   178
Psalm 22:18   179
Psalm 41:9   178
Psalm 82:6   178
Revelation   88
Revelation 1:10-16   84
Revelation 2:7   163
Revelation 2:11   163
Revelation 2:17   163
Revelation 2:26   163
Revelation 3:5   163

Revelation 3:12   163
Revelation 3:21   163
Revelation 5:9   26
Zechariah 12:8-11   179
Zechariah 12:10   179
Zechariah 9:9   178
Zechariah 13:1-2   179

# NAME INDEX

Aristotle  177
Baldwin, Dave  viii
Barton, Stephen C  177
Berkeley, George  98
Brinkley, Neale  2
Brook, Alison  viii
Carson, D A  73, 125, 170
Carson, Don  4
Chesterton, G K  79
Christie, Linford  85
Clare, Prof Anthony  116
Dummett, Des  viii
Galileo  171, 176-177
Gillray, James  152
Gleick, James  171
Graham, Billy  116
Gray, Tony  viii
Hornal, Alistair  viii
Irons, Jeremy  115
Just SJ, Rev Dr Felix  4, 67
Layard, Richard  95
Lewis, C S  77
Lowe, Dr Ivan & Margaret  71
Maria Celeste, Sister  176
Maslow  147, 154
McDonald Bailey  85
McNamara, Jo  viii
Molton, Dee  viii
Moody, D L  149
Moses, Ed  84
Newton  171
Nicholl, Colin  90
Nix, Garth  14

Patel, Dev  115
Radcliffe, Paula  85
Ryle, J C  4
Shakespeare  152
Sobel, Dava  171, 176
Suchet, David  2
Wells, Alan  85
Whitefield, George  149
Wilkinson, David  177
Williams, Rowan  89
Wilson, A N  177
Young, Dani  viii, 22, 51, 83, 112, 186

# Making sense of Romans
## When You Read it for Yourself

It has been about 500 years since Christians used a new technology – the printing press – to bring God's Word to everyone, and they changed the world. These days, we do less private Bible study than our predecessors although we have more and better resources. What if we studied the Bible the way we diagnosed our coughs, pursued our hobbies, or learned to cook lasagne?

*Making Sense of Romans* encourages us to use the internet more in Bible study and offers a simple framework – the faith story, the hope story and the love story – for anyone to find their way into Romans. Over 13 chapters it can be used to teach Romans from the pulpit in a quarter, or as a home group series. The style is easy-reading verging on chatty, to approach the messages of Romans in fresh ways, with questions at the end of each chapter which can be used for individual or group study. Available at

*www.wordsbydesign.co.uk*